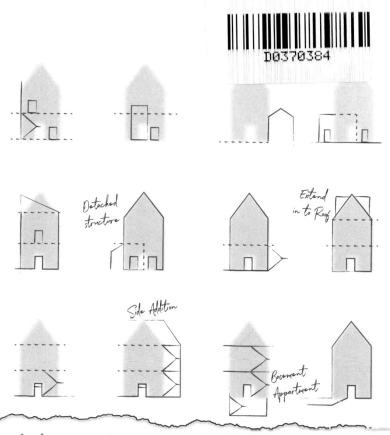

Housing for Humans

A Book to Imagine, Create and Design a New
Housing Model in America

ileana schinder

HOUSING FOR HUMANS

First published in 2021 by

Panoma Press Ltd
48 St Vincent Drive, St Albans, Herts, AL1 5SJ, UK
info@panomapress.com
www.panomapress.com

Book layout by Neil Coe.

978-1-784529-54-3

Dedication

To Wayne, my harbor

To my parents Alicia and Raul, my wings

To my children Veronica and Julian, you are the wind

Acknowledgements

This book was only possible thanks to those who showed love, support, and humor to the process. My husband Wayne, who with wit, love, and warm scones on Sunday mornings gave me the energy to carry on. To Julian and Veronica who came along for ice cream every step of the way. To my sister Guillermina and my parents Alicia and Raul, who always picked up the phone and let me talk about what I was trying to do, their encouragement from Argentina was the strength I needed, in Spanish, naturally.

To my friends who read early copies of the book and gave me feedback that helped me carry on: Paige Morimoto, Joyce Yin, and Colleen Cancio.

To my business advisors from HerCorner, Frederique Campagne Irwin, and Kimberly Berger, you showed me how to look at the navigation tools in this boat that is called architecture, during every storm and sunny day.

The organizations that inspired me to write this book and the people who work there, Coalition for Smarter Growth, Habitat for Humanity, and United Planning Organization. To my team, Nadeje Fuller and Kelly Ehrlich. Because of your hard work and wild spirit, this book was also possible.

Gracias.

Contents

Introduction – How We Got Here

The first time I watched *Home Alone* I was a 14-year-old growing up in Argentina. Back then, the idea of America with houses so big you could lose your children in them seemed fun but also perfectly plausible. I watched the movie again with my own children during Christmas of 2020. As an architect, an immigrant and a mom navigating a year of loss and isolation, I wondered about what home had become: for architects, for movies, for immigrants, for families.

My years as a residential architect in Washington, DC gave me signs on what is the new normal, but why is it still so challenging to discuss what housing is? Who deserves it and who can afford it, who can age in it and who can profit from it?

In the years I have designed homes I have seen a pattern: most of my commissions were about carving out space for new modes of housing. Most families reaching out to me wanted better and more sustainable spaces for their new, growing, and aging families. Families looking for housing today are so different from the ones in the Hollywood movies I grew up watching.

It seems that the ideal houses we were made to believe in are fading away. More innovative options that allow for flexibility, sustainability, multigenerational approaches, and financial support are the new norm. From my perspective as an architect, I enjoy watching how the home has transformed from a financial transaction to the stage where a new model of family can thrive.

This book is an exploration of that discovery. It is the result of years of changing dank basements into family rooms, of converting abandoned garages into additional dwelling units. I may not have had a commission so big where you can lose a child in the attic but, instead, my projects have welcomed older generations, added rental income, and brought spaces to life. I researched this book to learn why. This book explores how we got here: that a country so vast and rich could have looked away from a looming housing crisis that reached humanitarian proportions from coast to coast.

Language has always been my playground, it helped me discover words in English that did not exist in my native Spanish (sherbet!). Language and design have always carried me in the process to project houses. This tango taught me that in America, the term "single-family house" carries a cultural and economic load that could not be translated into Spanish. When it comes to homes and culture, it seemed that the rest of the American housing types were relegated to some ascetic description: apartment, condo, duplex, townhouse. I also discovered that there were no words to describe a housing type that had existed for ages: the additional dwelling unit. As if any format aside from the suburban model needed an explanation to be fully understood.

My immigrant's English is still sometimes filled with misnomers: popsicle for ice cream, stairs for ladders, and hard hats for helmets. It is never more evident than when I mix the words for house and home. And yet, I am still learning that in America there is always room for innovation and creativity, and improved language skills. My own discovery of language for writing this book may give the keys to others to look around and rethink their options for home.

This book is my exploration as an architect and an immigrant on how the American housing crisis came to be, how layers and generations of zoning, financial and cultural waves built and demolished concepts of housing and family models.

This book gives space to everyone else that has questioned where and how to call their place home. This book makes room to house those who cannot drive, who struggle to find a place to thrive, who want something different from the unrealistic models we have built so far.

This book gives permission to rethink our idea of home: where to build it, how to occupy it, and most importantly, why to design the way we do. This book is about houses and the people who live in them.

This book is about housing for humans.

CHAPTER 1

About Urban Housing

Housing options enhance the potential to engage in civic life because the dynamic between public and private spaces organizes social opportunities. The built environment is the stage for a shared social wealth.

Through each economic crisis and weighted by environmental awareness, there is a cultural acceptance about living with less. Traditional large homes in low-density settings increase the distance between services. In fact, the types of housing we have are part of the housing deficiency at all levels: the overabundance of homogeneous housing is socially, racially, and economically exclusionary. The relationship between zoning regulations and lack of innovative housing options has cemented the current crisis in affordable housing.

The predominance of single-family home zoning regulations challenge access to affordable housing for a significant proportion of the population. Single-family homes demand income, time, and physical ability to maintain them. From a livability perspective, this typology also emphasizes a car-dependent culture. And yet, the cultural and historical value of this type of housing misrepresents the current American family model. Innovative housing types, like additional dwelling units, add economic value and contribute new housing options for a changing society.

The current homogeneous existing housing stock excludes large swaths of the population: the elderly, disabled, and the poor. Designed and built for the nuclear family model of the mid-20th century, the typical single-family home in America is a poor match to the current cultural and economic model of a family unit today. And yet, today we buy, inhabit, and pay for the homes as if life has not significantly changed from previous generations. Not only are houses too big, too far away from each other but they are also too inflexible to adapt to the environment, household format, and economic reality of families in the 21st century.

The right size of home

Each home contains and reflects cultural and family dynamism. I have experienced this with a large number of design projects that demanded better space for new stages in life. Every project that arrives at my studio has become an adaptation to current urban and family demands. They seem intimately unique but, put together, they reflect a pattern for new housing types within the established urban environments.

A few years ago, when a client called my office in Washington, DC, the design project was different from what I used to assume the typical architecture commission should have been. Instead of adding new space or modernizing a kitchen, she wanted to make her Capitol Hill home smaller. She loved the house, the neighborhood it sat in, and the proximity to friends and shopping. And yet, after becoming a widow, she felt that the house was too big for her. Her goal in the new stage of life was to have more time hiking in the Blue Ridge Mountains and visiting friends.

But how do you make a house smaller? The project consisted of subdividing the home to transform the bottom part of her townhouse into a studio apartment. The income generated by the new unit was a means to support her lifestyle as she aged, through travel instead of material goods.

Projects like this illustrate how the subdivision of existing homes is the design undercurrent for every generation to revisit their need for housing. In every age group, the physical environment is crucial to support an enriching lifestyle. The shape, location, and design of a home welcomes others as an urban support system with economic and social benefits.

The value of walking and biking to local amenities is also a strong trend to revisit the size of housing. Living close to others allows for an economic supportive network in the neighborhood, from the local corner store to a dentist's practice. Far from high-density neighborhoods where high-rise buildings define the streetscape, local neighborhoods have room to grow within backyards, basements, and alleys. There is a missing density in our current housing typology, the kind that supports local businesses and services. Smaller homes in shared lots have the power to contribute options to a population rarely served in the current market, from renters to retirees.

Making room

The current housing deficit is not the result of lack of space. In fact, sustainable and affordable housing is the result of a supportive environment that accommodates all physical and emotional needs for the people who occupy them. The highlight on living smaller is popular in TV shows and books with a focus on tiny homes and tight living quarters. This oversimplified idea "just less" only allows for a fringe lifestyle that is feasible for a small proportion of the population for a limited period of time.

When walking the dog through my neighborhood in Washington, DC, I see abandoned garages, sheds, and old workshops. These buildings, served by alleys, are currently housing stuff instead of people. Originally planned and built for small industrial businesses, the structures now sit empty. This image is almost universal in the United States today, space and buildings dedicated to stuff and cars instead of people.

Market trends, habit, and investment potential reinforce the rigidity and disconnection between private and public spaces. The pandemic of 2020 has driven homeowners to revisit how each space is designed, used, and connected to others. The intensity of use of private space, along with the reconfiguration of the public realm, adds a new layer of the understanding of human occupancy of the built environment.

Compact home design, with true insight of how and how often a room is used, has become essential to understand a new culturally acceptable size of a home. What used to be the guest room is now the office. What used to be the basement is now an apartment. What used to be the garage is now the outdoor school building for kids studying at home. What used to be a street is now a street-eatery. The pandemic of 2020 was the catalyst to accelerate and emphasize changes of use of public and private spaces.

Compact, urban, and innovative housing typologies are the new normal. In fact, as an architect, when I started my own practice I did not expect that the biggest share of my portfolio would be under my feet. The past 10 years in Washington, DC has seen a transformation of the use of basements. Low demand for housing in the previous 50 years abandoned lower levels of existing townhouses, as housing demand increased, basements were transformed into living spaces, like family rooms and apartments. Old basements are being transformed to house people instead of stuff.

The projects I have worked on express the increased desire to share and contribute private property to the public housing stock. This mix of housing sizes also adds cultural wealth in the shared experiences in public areas. Traditionally, retail had the physical space and social bonds to the neighborhoods they served, but low-density suburban housing and current zoning regulations makes them unfeasible today. Heterogeneous housing types in close proximity also encourages the development of businesses that strengthen the local economy.

Large swaths of homogeneous housing also emphasize the division of rich and poor urban districts. The redistribution of public services and available affordable housing have the capacity to stimulate equity in the use of the city. Diversity in housing sizes and types promotes community bonds through a common experience of the public realm, from schools to parks. The existing housing stock has the transformative capability to become the solution of the current housing deficit.

CHAPTER 2

The Shape of Zoning

We cannot talk about housing unless we also talk about zoning. How we organize, place, and value urban housing is heavily regulated by guidelines set by each city. Zoning profiles the city by a system of economic and cultural values of the land, private and public. It also organizes the city uses, such as residential or industrial. Even if some compatible uses overlap, in general, traditional zoning methods strictly organize the city by single-use areas.

How zoning shaped housing

I used to believe that architects and planners were the main influences on the shape of the city as if the urban experience could be sculpted by design. Until I learned that one of the most influential factors in housing shortage today was not designed but decreed by law. In fact, one of the first zoning regulations stemmed from a legal dispute about housing typology and its location.

Heavily influenced by the racist and economic framework of the time, the 1923 United States Supreme Court ruled the implementation of single-family home zoning using the concept of "quality of life" as an argument to reshape cities across the land. In their argument, apartment buildings were labeled as "parasites," generators of "disturbing noises" and "depriving children of the privilege of quiet." The view of pastoral America we experience today was paved a century ago with this perception that single-family homes were better for Americans than other housing typologies. This view of access to housing heavily dependent on income and race highlighted the current inequality of access to housing and services that American minorities still suffer from today.

How much do zoning rules affect housing access today? San Francisco in California still dedicates 82% of all residential land to single-family homes, leaving only 18% for other housing formats, such as apartments or duplexes. Seattle, in Washington, has 75% of its residential land "single-family use," putting a small percentage of land able to meet other housing needs.

In the last decade, in an effort to mitigate this division of housing types by zone as a factor in the current housing deficit, cities and states have attempted to ban single-family home zoning.

The history of zoning

Zoning regulations organize urban life by shaping buildings. It arranges setbacks from streets and massing shapes, from lot occupancy to usage. These regulations are extremely local, and each jurisdiction sets their own rules based on its history and projected future growth. Changing zoning rules has social, political and, most importantly, economic consequences for the city and private citizens.

The first zoning regulations in the United States were set in the 1920s when the Commerce Department drafted a model of zoning ordinances that made it easier for states to establish their own local zoning laws. In fact, New York became the first city to implement this type of zoning law. Until then, even if there were masterplans based on ideal city models, those plans lacked regulatory mechanisms through guidelines for developers and private citizens. The application of single-use zoning shaped cities and resulted in dense urban cores surrounded by low-density residential suburbs. With time, those suburbs filled with low-density residential zones surrounded by large gardens and wide streets.

This government planning of American cities was set in the context of heavy industrialization, large migration from rural to urban areas, and development of railroads that expanded cities. Even as job compensation improved significantly during the 1920s, poverty also increased along with urban crime. The shape of the city was fundamental to prioritize the location, size, and accessibility to the private and public space.

Aside from the physical shaping of the city, zoning regulations early in the 20th century reflected the racist approach to land ownership, value, and occupancy. The first official use of zoning as a regulator of the use of private land by the government has its roots in the Elmwood neighborhood of Berkeley, California. In 1916, the city leaders intended to segregate white homeowners from apartment complexes occupied by minority residents. The ruling prohibited the construction of anything other than one home per lot. Because of the values of the properties, this restriction made it difficult for people of color to purchase or lease property in the same neighborhoods. Even today, this pattern of mandated minimum sizes for housing is a method that excludes poorer citizens from having access to homeownership in desirable neighborhoods. More than 100 years later, about 49% of available land for residential uses in Berkeley is still dedicated to single-family homes.

The example of Berkeley became a model for other jurisdictions to include racial and economic exclusions to housing developments throughout the country early in the 20th century. The consequence of this approach can be seen today in lower level of homeownership for minorities, lower value for their properties, and clustered neighborhoods based on race.

On the East Coast, a racist approach to zoning and housing development is also evident in the urban history of Arlington, Virginia as a sample of other cities in America. Research shows that 71% of the land is dedicated to single-family homes today.

Even if America enjoyed strong and steady growth in the 1920s, after the market crash of October 1929 the economic damage to cities was significant in the collapse of the private sector construction industry.

Until that period, Arlington had been a fast-growing streetcar suburb. Early urban growth in the city had been in the form of bungalows and rowhouses. But because local leaders intended to preserve its original suburban character, a local ordinance banned townhouses in 1938, and remained in place until the 1960s. Increased housing segregation was exacerbated by race-based ordinances; around the 1930s, it was common to find covenants with exclusions for residential occupancy: it was illegal to inhabit a residence unless the occupant was a "person[s] of the Caucasian Race."

Even after the 1948 landmark U.S. Supreme Court case Shelley vs Kraemer that deemed racially restrictive covenants to be unconstitutional, discrimination against minorities in the sale and occupation of homes remained prevalent in Arlington and other parts of the country until the Fair Housing Act of 1968.

Shelley vs Kraemer was a landmark U.S. Supreme Court case that struck down racially restrictive housing covenants. The case arose after the Shelley family purchased a home in St Louis, Missouri, in a neighborhood with restricted covenants that prevented "people of the Negro or Mongolian race" from occupying the property. The Shelley family was African American. A neighbor, Louis Kramer who was white, sued to prevent the Shelleys from gaining possession of the property. The Supreme Court held that the racially restrictive agreements cannot enforce judicial enforcement of those covenants. Simply spoken, the racist covenants were constitutional but not enforceable by law.

It was not until 1968 that the Fair Housing Act outlawed housing discrimination. It was set up as a follow up from the Civil Rights Act of 1964: Title VIII prohibited discrimination concerning the sale, rental, and financing of housing based on race, religion, national origin, and sex. The day of the Senate vote – April 4th – the civil rights leader Martin Luther King was assassinated in Memphis, Tennessee. The Fair Housing Act passed on April 10th and President Johnson signed it into law the following day.

Decades of racist zoning practices have concrete impacts on vulnerable populations today. By 1950, 95% of the Arlington population identified as white. African Americans and other non-whites were forced to find housing in existing African American communities within the county or move outside of Arlington. Even if from 1980 to 2010 Arlington became more ethnically diverse, most growth of racially diverse areas occurred where housing diversification and transit had developed during the second half of the 20th century. However, areas that saw the least racial and economic diversity were those with the most single-family detached homes.

How zoning can change: from Oregon to Minneapolis

Innovation in zoning regulations has the potential to undo its history of housing overregulation and increase innovative options. An example of this change was implemented by the Oregon legislature in 2019 by passing a bill that banned single-family homes from the state, spearheading a trend that is multiplying across the country. The Oregon bill requires that cities with more than 10,000 people allow duplexes in areas traditionally zoned exclusively for single-family homes. The city of Portland also allows for denser housing types such as quadruplexes and "cottage clusters." Cottage clusters are dwelling units organized around a common yard.

Minneapolis in Minnesota has moved in the same direction as a way to mitigate the housing crisis exacerbated by the low-density result of single-family home zones. City officials gave a legal framework to form-based housing when they banned single-family home zoning in 2019. Even if it is still legal to build a single home in a lot, it is also legal to develop duplex and triplexes in most of the city.

Engrained support for the zoning status quo has created a housing crisis of humanitarian proportions throughout

America. Changes to zoning regulation are a politically charged process and resistance to the adjustment in well-established neighborhoods is always tense. The concerns range from traffic to school overcrowding. There is a myth that a change from single-family home to form-shaped residential uses will devalue properties. However, increased density in existing single-family home zones introduces innovative housing types that satisfy modern economic and cultural needs for a large portion of the population.

Upzoning: from California and Washington, DC

Upzoning is the process of increasing zoning density in a neighborhood by converting single residential lots into multifamily properties.

An example of state level upzoning can be seen in California in 2019. To mitigate the impact of high housing costs, Governor Gavin Newsom signed five bills that regulated homeowners' rights to develop additional dwelling units in their properties. The bill made most historical local and state housing restrictions obsolete. The new regulation facilitates the development of new dwelling units within existing residential properties.

Traditionally used to discourage innovative development of housing, the building permitting process in many jurisdictions tends to be an obscure and subjective process that adds costs and uncertainty. The new California regulation sets limits on how long reviewers could delay the approval of plans. Most importantly, it sets limits on how long an additional dwelling unit building permit could be held for review by any jurisdiction. After 60 days, if not resolved by local reviewers, the additional dwelling unit will be considered approved.

Another method that jurisdictions use to discourage the development of adding dwelling units in the existing residential context is the owner occupancy requirement. Even in jurisdictions where additional units are allowed, this requirement mandates that the owner must occupy one of the dwellings. This requirement reduces the ability to create more units within rental properties and discourages owners from adding a unit because it forces them to sell the property if they want or need to move. In California, since 2019 the new zoning proposal also removed owner occupancy requirements.

Another method that zoning rules has to ensure that single-family home zones remain intact is to require off-street parking. By over prescribing parking needs in residential neighborhoods, zoning regulations can ensure that most lots will not have the area or frontage to supply oversized parking requirements when additional dwelling units are in place. Also, requiring off-street parking at properties eligible for additional dwelling units prevents many homeowners from converting garages into housing, one of the easiest ways to transform existing structures into dwellings. In California, the new law removed parking requirements if the properties are half a mile from public transit.

Permitting fees for additional dwelling units is a tool used by certain jurisdictions to prevent the development of new units. The California bill also limits greatly how much and what types of fees can be charged to add a unit to an existing property. Because impact fees discourage the creation of alternative housing, this new regulation limits impact fees based on the smaller unit to be generated.

This new zoning regulation also sets restrictions on the ability of homeowners' associations (HOA) to ban or overregulate the creation of additional dwelling units. In California, as in most of the United States, large portions of single-family homes are ready to provide additional housing but are banned from doing so from their homeowner's association rules. Traditionally, homeowners' associations oppose the transformation of their single-family homes into any use, no matter the social or economic circumstances of the residents.

There are more than 350,000 homeowners' associations in America, representing about 40 million homeowners. That means about 53% of all homes in the United States. In the 1960s, riding on the post-war housing boom, homeownership was associated to attain financial stability. Even if racist covenants were deemed unenforceable, the first HOAs were formed as new planned communities explored how they could exclude "undesirables" from their projects and avoid getting sued. Even though the Fair Housing Act prevented most kinds of rampant racial discrimination, the damage to equal access to housing had been done.

Today most homeowners' associations police private features like aesthetic choices, enforce minor behavior violations, and restrict architectural features – interior or exterior – that prevent the implementation of additional dwelling units. By allowing new dwellings within areas regulated by HOA, affordable and innovative housing can be distributed in a wider area currently low-density and off-limits to renters.

Barriers to create new housing in the United States limit the capacity that each homeowner has to create dwellings within their property. The example of California had a direct impact on the housing supply: after it partially opened additional dwelling units' regulations in 2017, one in five total housing building permits were for these units. In 2018 alone, 6,000 additional dwelling units were created. This number doubled in 2019, reaching almost 16,000. Before the new law had passed, the number of applications in 2015 for additional dwelling units had been 225.

But the crisis in housing options is not just about numbers. The 2019 California zoning change also shifted the areas where the additional dwelling units occurred. These projects are currently appearing in neighborhoods accessible to transit occupied by people who are first-time homeowners. Of those units created, 92% were built in zones originally parceled as "single-family residential" before the law passed.

The potential for change in housing options in California seems unlimited. San Jose alone has existing capacity to create additional dwelling units in 120,000 lots. In the San Francisco Bay Area, the availability of lots that can provide an additional dwelling unit is 1 million.

California's crisis in affordable housing was manufactured by historic local overregulation and forcing low-density housing in areas where population grew and diversified. The evolution on the laws that regulated additional dwelling units created a new potential for existing homeowners to become housing entrepreneurs in their own backyard. Because the crisis of affordable housing has reached a national level, innovative zoning in California has paved the way on how to remove barriers at a state level that will contribute positive housing changes at local level.

Existing zoning regulations throughout the country, and the lengthy process to change them, perpetuate the invisible reach of housing inequality. Zoning maps are a political tool that reinforces rules of economic and racial discrimination.

Despite the efforts to create more and innovative housing options, as of 2020, in the San Francisco Bay Area, 83% of the residential land is still dedicated to single-family housing, San Jose 94%, and Los Angeles 75%. Less than a quarter of the residential areas of those cities can take apartments or denser types of housing. California's home prices are higher than anywhere else in the United States and it faces an accelerating housing catastrophe affecting its social and economic sustainability in the long term.

The trend of rising housing costs began in the 1970s and continues today. Housing costs in California in 2020 were two-and-a-half times the average national home price.

Zoning changes at a local level also changes the involvement of homeowners and those who design the homes. I experienced the impact of a zoning change in Washington, DC as I explored new design options for my own architecture practice. Instead of expensive residential renovations and additions, many clients wanted to dedicate a portion of their house to be rented out. Before the 2016 revision of the zoning code, accessory apartments were highly restricted and subject to approval from the Board of Zoning Adjustment, a lengthy process with unpredictable results. Because the new code removed administrative barriers to the process and increased the potential for units, most of my potential clients were eager to convert unused basements and garages into housing.

The popularity of additional dwelling units in Washington, DC had been in the core of the city since the beginning. In fact, until the 20th century, the city had a network of alleyways and basement apartments that were the source of housing options for servants. The assumption was that middle and upper classes lived on the street while servants and the lower class faced the alleys. But because alley housing was considered unsanitary, Congress banned the construction of new alley dwellings in 1892. From 3,300 alley dwellings surveyed in 1912, only 108 structures survived by 2016.

In 2016, fueled by high demand for housing and rising cost of living, the modification of the zoning code in Washington, DC allowed for by-right developments of accessory apartments in most residential zones of the city. These new dwellings allow homeowners to add a new rental property to their existing home: existing garages and basements became the source of new housing to mitigate high housing costs. Despite this effort, Washington, DC remains the 7th most expensive city in the country to own a home and the 8th to rent.

California and Washington, DC, among many other cities in the country, illustrate that the modernization in zoning rules has a positive economic impact on homeowners and renters. From available units to financial contribution, zoning regulations have the capacity to organize equitable access to housing.

Traditional and form-based zoning on the East Coast

So how does zoning affect housing? Current zoning maps organize the city by use. Most zoning maps envision people who live, work, and play in separate places. This method to organize the city has proven to be expensive and inaccessible to many. Lifestyle changes, mostly in work and shopping habits, have made implemented zoned maps obsolete. We work from home more frequently and shop online with more intensity than ever. Travel time between activities has lost significance and quality. Separating zoning maps by use alone wastes space and excludes individuals who do not drive.

A better zoning approach promotes an urban environment shaped by buildings but also enriched by a healthy mix of uses. Different types and sizes of housing units in close proximity has the capacity to support retail, such as corner stores and professional services. The pandemic of 2020 reassessed working conditions and emphasized the potential of alternative housing typologies as a catalyst for economic change.

The traditional zoning format that shaped the cities we live in is known in North America as the Euclidean zoning model. The name comes from a 1926 court case in Euclid, Ohio and it has been the dominant zoning system since. The resolution of that landmark case gave the government the power to limit and exclude uses from private property. So, what happened in 1926 that matters today? Ambler Realty owned 68 acres in Euclid, Ohio, a suburb of Cleveland. In an attempt to prevent the industrial Cleveland from changing the character of the village, it developed a zoning ordinance that banned the development of land dedicated to industrial uses. Because Amber Realty saw its properties in Euclid devalued, it sued the village arguing that the government limits on use was a financial burden for them, the landowners.

The Supreme Court sided with the village of Euclid, stating the zoning ordinances was a reasonable extension of the village's police power. With its resolution, the court gave power to local jurisdictions to regulate the private use of land. After 1926, the United States saw an explosion in zoning ordinances that are the norm today.

Aside from the Euclidian mode of single-use zone to outline the city, form-based zoning organizes the public space by shape instead of by use. Form-based codes respond to the physical structure of a community to promote better pedestrian environments. An early example of this approach to urban planning can be seen in the New York's 1916 Zoning resolution. This regulation mandated setbacks of tall buildings to allow access to natural light to neighboring structures. These mathematical formulas based on height and lot size shaped many early skyscrapers admired today. Every trip I take to New York City I admire the capacity of the city to hold in close proximity offices, apartments, retail, and professional services all within walking distance. Buildings follow a pattern of development – impressively high! – but they do not mandate who can use them and how.

The difference between single-use and form-based zoning approach to established residential zones provides new opportunities to reduce housing deficit. Under form-based zoning, two identical houses can comprise a variety of interior layouts that accommodate multiple dwelling units. For example, neighboring structures with identical façade and mass can serve different family types. One can provide a single-family home while the other can be subdivided into multiple levels. This expression means that both buildings contribute to neighborhood character. From the outside, both buildings are residential, but from the inside, each structure welcomes different types of families, in size, income, and lifestyle.

Urban density vs urban intensity

Zoning organizes the city by shape and use, the resulting buildings create density. Density is a mathematical formula that illustrates the amount of development per acre permitted, and it is measured as dwelling units per acre. Different housing types make up residential density, for example, single-family homes can fit, at most, 12 units per acre. Townhouses can be accommodated up to 24 per acre, walk-up apartments 30 units per acre, and higher buildings above 40 units per acre.

However, density alone does not tell the complete story of urban and suburban housing. Density can be visible or invisible. Visible density is the public expression of a structure, be it a single-family home or an apartment building facing the street. Invisible density blends in with the neighborhood character. A dwelling in the rear of the property, basement apartments, and the subdivision of an existing building are examples of invisible density. Visible density modifications are feasible near high-transit corridors, such as high traffic roads and train stations. Invisible density modifications, as a contributor to new dwelling units, can be implemented within the existing fabric of the city.

Density is a concept of land use planning that behaves like a statistic of performance, but it is an inadequate tool to measure housing quality and availability. Current rigid zoning regulations prevent the intermixing of smaller affordable units within the established context of single-family homes. Invisible density contributes housing units by adapting the current housing stock through additions, housing subdivisions, and the reorganization of units within existing properties.

Urban density is measurable; it creates a mathematical figure that describes dwellings per acre. However, it is urban intensity that describes the experience of the urban environment. Urban intensity measures the resulting quality of the space that makes the city livable.

Density is easy to measure: it is a simple ratio of structures over land. Urban intensity, however, is the psychological and social dimension of the built environment. Urban intensity is evaluated by activity and its potential for social interaction. Intense places are attractive to individuals of different backgrounds because they stimulate economic, social, and cultural wealth. Expanding from the simplistic concept of urban density, the intentional design of the city and housing types enrich urban intensity.

Urban intensity also fosters a sense of personal safety and shared purpose. Jane Jacobs, in her book *The Death and Life of Great American Cities* (1961) highlighted the concept of "eyes on the street" in which each individual adds to a sense of security and belonging. It is the crowd of people that prevents danger. According to Jacobs, the key to a rich urban experience is the mix of strangers sharing the public space.

I was raised in Argentina, where "eyes on the street" was a daily experience. It was common to be asked to go the local corner store when my mom was missing an ingredient for lunch. For an eight-year-old in the 1980s, it was liberating to cross two streets holding the money, greet the shopkeeper, and come back with whatever I was asked to buy, along with a few pieces of candy instead of change. Coming to America, I noticed that the distance, physical and intellectual, between residential and retail condition the experience of the public space for people of different ages and physical abilities. It is no wonder that my favorite children's book today is Mo Willems' *Nanette's Baguette* in which the main character walks by herself to buy a baguette for the first time. Many decades later, I still look for bakeries when I visit a new city as a sign of healthy urban design.

Communal "eyes on the street" occurs when collective activities, asynchronous and concurrent, share the built environment. Shopping, education, exercise, and entertainment are contributors to neighborhood safety and increased sense of belonging. Individual participation in public activities depends on the capacity of each neighbor to reach them by foot, bicycle, and car. The frequency and intensity of use of public spaces also depends on the number of people that are engaged in participating. Affordable housing options available in established neighborhoods has the potential to increase urban intensity with gentle density.

Heterogeneous housing types clustered within neighborhoods promotes asynchronous use of the public space. That is, the promotion of use of the space and services during different times of the day and the week. A park surrounded by large and small homes attracts users based on age. Small children may use the playground during the day, older adults may use it to exercise early in the morning. However, homogeneous housing distribution creates dormitory zones where high intensity of activities during narrow times of the day creates an artificial demand for space: oversized parking lots, wide traffic paths, and peak-hour demands for services.

A healthy mix of housing types within a neighborhood fosters a balanced use of the public realm during the day and night. It also increases safety by providing "eyes on the street" and allows for right-sizing infrastructure. Heterogeneous housing also reduces car dependency as the main factor to participate in the public space. Innovative housing layouts can contribute to the local economy and a balanced approach to urban design influenced by work from home options, along with a dispersion in private enterprises in residential neighborhoods.

Planning: a brief history

So how did American cities get here? Historically the city was organized though the natural needs of those who inhabited it: retail, housing, and industries were located as demand arose. However, the modern origins of urban planning appeared at the end of the 19th century as a reaction to the over industrialization of the city. Concerned with sanitation, transportation, and provision of goods and services, urban planners became concerned with quality of life and the value of land. After all, the goal of modern urban planning is the recognition of the public interest in the common urban spaces by balancing physical design, land use, and social sciences.

In the early 20th century, the replacement of horses with motorized vehicles became the most influential change in the shape and growth of the city. This technology allowed for territorial expansion and increased distances between workers and jobs along with the fast movements of goods, from production to market. This shift of urban movement congested old layout of cities, like London, Paris, and New York in the early 1900s.

In fact, more than 50 manufacturers of cars were part of New York City and its surrounding areas. The Allen was one of the earliest cars built in the city and it had chain-driven wheels, like a motorcycle. Even if only one Allen survives today, the impact of all those vehicles in the urban expression of the city remains strong today.

Transportation created such an impact on urban living that the first efforts to establish planning departments appeared in the 1900s to organize the public space for common benefit. The first recognized planning agency in the United States was created in Hartford, Connecticut in 1907. Prior to this, planning commissions were disbanded once a plan had been developed. The origins of city planning intended to preserve property values and achieve an economic efficiency in the urban layout. These early planning agencies divided the city by uses of incompatible activities and set patterns of circulation.

Aside from its early government developments, one of the most significant changes in the history of planning and zoning in America occurred after World War II. During that period, high demand for housing stimulated the construction of suburban developments. Privately planned and financed, the federal government provided tax relief for homeowners and government-guaranteed mortgages. Today's urban sprawl is the result of that type of planning. Paired with land clearance and the implementation of public housing in the city, local governments played a significant role in the disinvestment of urban cores. It included the dispersion of housing opportunities, reduction of educational institutions and eroded business opportunities away from historically established urban cores.

By the 1950s, the focus of residential growth was placed on the supply of low-density, single-family detached housing as the most prevalent typology of the growing middle class of the time. That cultural impact on housing and family models is ubiquitous even today. This physical division between people's needs, from housing to education, from healthcare to entertainment, contributed to individual car dependency for transportation. This type of development, academically described as "conventional suburban development," has always been known as "sprawl."

The first significant shift in the understanding of urban planning appeared in the 1980s with the concept of New Urbanism. This approach introduced the idea of walkable neighborhoods as the host of a wide range of housing and job types. This understating of design and public policy also promotes mixing uses and universal access to public spaces as a way to support diversity and equity. Strategies of New Urbanism result in the reduction of traffic, balanced development of housing and jobs, and set up the context to increase the availability of affordable housing.

Even if early New Urbanist developments were implemented in greenfield sites, such as Seaside in Florida, the principle of mixed uses and prioritizing pedestrian amenities resulted in rich high-quality urban environments. In fact, another new urbanist project, Kentlands in Maryland, not only incorporated alleys but also added small quarters above the garage of single-family homes. Many of the projects throughout the country materialize the premise of New Urbanism, which adds emphasis to mixed uses, housing variety, and pedestrian access for all. Not too different from the design premises of urban planning before the 1950s.

The real impact of zoning regulations

The pandemic of 2020 has exposed the shortcomings of historic and outdated zoning rules as the organizer of daily life. Battered by the novel coronavirus, homes became workplaces, businesses, and schools. These short-term measures turned neighborhoods into hubs of activity during the day, strengthening the use of public space during off-peak hours. Zones labeled as "residential" became both a source of shelter and its own engine of economic dynamic.

So, what would happen if this restructuring of residential zones were to stay? From a dentist to a physical therapist, from a yoga studio to an ice cream parlor, the city has an existing residential infrastructure that can accommodate dormitory functions and daily activities. Barriers for this new neighborhood economic dynamic remain banned by outdated zoning regulations: you cannot open a yoga studio, but you can build a three-car garage in your backyard. Effectively forcing all the yoga students to drive to a location outside of the neighborhood, while all the garages are empty during the yoga class.

Some cities noticed the 2020 conversion of neighborhoods from single use residential to mixed use areas, and implemented timely changes to their zoning rules. The work from home demands brought by the pandemic drove the Board of Supervisors in Fairfax County in Virginia to make a significant change in their zoning and business regulations. They removed zoning barriers for residents to operate a business inside their homes as a long-term measure. Despite the opposition of some homeowners' groups, the Board of Supervisors lowered the cost of licenses for home-based businesses, like a beauty salon or a dentist practice. The home-based business license fee was reduced by 97%, from $16,375 to $435.

The new allowance for residential business still limits the number of customers that can visit the shop to two at a time and a maximum of six per day. So, in anticipation of neighborhood complaints, new parking regulations require one on-site parking spot for those premises that will operate a business at home. The example in Fairfax, VA shows how to revisit historic zoning regulations that adapt to current economic realities. This innovation in zoning and bureaucracy during a crisis has the potential to foster local growth and support contemporary local needs.

Not only did Fairfax see the need to innovate their business approach to residential neighborhoods but they also eased the permit application process to create additional dwelling units. New housing types, distributed among new neighborhood businesses, create new economic and social bonds in the local market. The last time Fairfax revised their zoning rules had been in 1979.

Current rules that overregulate uses in residential neighborhoods, from housing to businesses, hinder progress and weaken local economies. The existing housing stock has the capacity to contribute to neighborhood health when outdated zoning rules revisit regulations on parking, businesses, and accessory dwellings. Low-density and low-intensity services can be better distributed throughout the city and stimulate growth in smaller scale commercial hubs. My own architecture practice was started as a work from home format in 2014, in the Eckington neighborhood of Washington, DC, surrounded by townhouses.

Like most small businesses, my operation received few visitors, if any, during the day. Online communications today make operating a business from home even easier than a decade ago. However, outdated zoning rules continue to ban this practice in most jurisdictions. A healthy mix of low-intensity retail, offices, and homes creates economic synergy.

Outdated zoning regulations restrict how existing housing stock can be used and limit the availability of services within walking distance from those who need it. The internet makes more jobs accessible in distant places from expensive downtown real estate. Dentists, graphic designers, and other professionals can operate from buildings in already established residential neighborhoods with little conflict with neighbors. Sub-occupied industrial buildings, townhouses and existing freestanding garages in residential neighborhoods have the capacity to promote economic growth, create jobs, and support new business models.

Inclusionary zoning

Inclusionary zoning refers to planning ordinances that require a share of new construction to affordable by people with low to moderate incomes. The term intends to correct unfair historic zoning regulations and attempts to counteract old "exclusionary zoning" practices where market values prevent low-income residents from accessing property based on cost of housing.

Inclusionary zoning has the benefit of increasing the supply of affordable units for low-income families in zones where good employment and quality education is available. It also reduces the economic and racial segregation that results from homogeneous housing distribution. Despite its intended benefits, inclusionary zoning has resulted in a limited number of affordable units compared to other economic measures, such as housing vouchers.

Because inclusionary zoning in most cities is negotiable between developers and local politicians, the regional impact is limited and may not contribute to satisfy the regional deficit of affordable housing.

The influence of crises in urban design

The shock of the Covid-19 crisis has extended into urban and residential design. As I write this book, cities have turned sidewalks into outdoor restaurants, alternative transit options have increased, and families are questioning the choice of institutional residential options for the elderly. The contribution of indoor and outdoor design shaped the experience of a year of isolation and loss. However, this is not the first catastrophe to jolt the use of private and public space.

Throughout history, health crises impacted the shape of cities and homes. London welcomed outdoor public spaces surrounding the River Thames after the cholera outbreaks of the 19th century. In the same period, the heart of Paris was a source of disease and overcrowding that was transformed with wide boulevards designed by Baron Haussmann making it one of the most iconic cities in the world today. Those urban design changes were the result of public health measures to bring natural light and air to the urban cores.

Even the tuberculosis epidemic influenced architecture. The widespread use of antibiotics to treat tuberculosis did not start until the 1950s. Between 1810 and 1815, the disease accounted for more than 25% of the deaths in New York City. In fact, in 1900, it was the country's third most common cause of death. After the discovery of the tubercle bacillus in 1882, and germ theory was understood, medical professionals knew that isolation was key to prevent the spread of the disease. Fresh air and sunlight were a person's best hope for recovery. The standard of care for TB was environmental and the design and construction of specialized sanatoriums coincided with the advent of Modernism. Flat roofs, balconies, and light-painted rooms with large windows for ventilation was intended to cure ailments brought on by crowded cities. These sanatoriums with large windows, extensive decks, and flat roofs were inspirations for many architects of the modern movement.

The current impact of Covid-19 with its ramifications in the economy, design, lack of affordable housing, and the social construct of homes for isolation and support, will shape the contribution of shelter as a source of care for future generations.

CHAPTER 3

About Affordability

Affordable housing is the type of dwelling that is reasonably priced, with adequate quality and practical location for lower and middle-income households. Affordability is the result of a complex set of economic, social, and cultural factors, and the current crisis is emphasized by income inequality in certain geographic regions. Moreover, a combination of high housing costs and high debt level is another contribution to less access to affordable housing for urban dwellers.

Access to affordable and accessible housing is relevant because it provides dwellings for low-cost labor, and reduces transportation costs. Increased housing demand, low production of units, and overregulation of lands are factors that reduce access to housing for lower income families.

Increased housing demand

For most of history, cities have been a magnet of economic and cultural activity. Even today, cities remain attractive as a source of education and jobs. In 2010, the urban population of the United States reached 309 million people, from a mere 5.3 million in 1800. The U.S. population that lived in cities in 1800 was 8%, in 2010 the number reached 81%. Not only are more people living in cities but also they are more diverse than ever. The demand for urban housing continues to increase today as cities become more interesting and accommodating to people seeking economic opportunities, education, and services.

Even if the pressure on urban growth has not always been uniform throughout the decades, the interest in living close to cultural and economic engines remains true today. The Covid-19 pandemic, as other economic crises of the past, has reshaped urban living and the makeup of homes. A new distribution of residences throughout the city has the capacity to house the new economic and cultural reality of its citizens. The health crisis of 2020 brought to light the role of housing in the creation of new jobs, need for shelter, and educational hubs. During the beginning of the pandemic in March of 2020, homes were seen as sources of isolation but also played a fundamental role in each person's capacity to seek shelter and safety.

Not just seen as a financial asset, the pandemic shifted the role of home and how it contributes to family life and social bonds. Housing also highlighted the conditions of those who fell victim to the virus. Households that lived in overcrowded conditions had larger incidences and worse health outcomes than those who lived in less crowded conditions. Insecure housing environments affected educational and job opportunities. Not only did the pandemic highlight the health implication of housing but also the economic fallout may lead to an increase in evictions.

Cities have evolved as a magnet of jobs and economic opportunity. However, through exclusionary zoning and gentrification, urban areas have become cost prohibitive for large portions of the population. The current urban housing deficit weakens social connections between economic actors and the places where they work, play, and learn.

For a more civilized city

As an architect, it is almost too tempting to focus on buildings, looking at historic details and technical solutions of modern architecture. And yet, when thinking about the buildings that make up the city, I must remember that buildings are for people. All buildings, the old and the new, the modest and the rich, the significant and the homey, exist to house, heal, and entertain people. Buildings provide shelter, significance, and value to human life. To build the city is also to organize people's lives: who will occupy it, pay for it, maintain it, and look at it. Buildings are a service for those who inhabit the city.

Movement organizes life. A significant proportion of the city is made up of a network of streets, alleys, and roads. Even if cars are culturally significant, current spaces dedicated to vehicles condition the human capacity to thrive in the public realm. Today, the United States has 2 billion parking spaces, for about 250 million cars. The area dedicated to parking cars in the United States is larger than the area dedicated to housing people.

The current housing deficit is also exacerbated by the context in which affordable housing is created. Not only is affordable housing scarce in urban environments but those that exist tend to be surrounded by insufficient services, like low-performance schools, fewer transit alternatives, and food deserts.

Transformative missing middle

Cities have the capacity to develop alternative housing models in existing neighborhoods. Missing middle housing is the transformative concept developed by Daniel Parolek, in which more housing units are created within the existing urban context. Building types like duplexes and cottage courts, among other typologies, are called "missing" because they have typically been illegal to build since the mid-1940s. And "middle" because they sit in the middle of a range between a detached single-family home and apartment buildings.

This understanding of different housing types in close proximity to each other emphasizes the beneficial relationship of economic diversity of the urban population.

Families that occupy those homes do share public services, from libraries to schools and job opportunities. Today, most current zoning regulations in the country prevent different sized homes in close proximity to each other, and also ban economic activity integrated into residential neighborhoods.

An equitable distribution of housing in the urban environment is an opportunity for a fair distribution of jobs, services, and educational options. As demand for affordable housing increases, the current approach to create units is unsustainable and unjust. With innovation in zoning regulations, governments and citizens have the capacity to contribute to the development of more affordable housing, from apartments in high-rises and granny flats in backyards. A healthy distribution of housing options throughout the city contributes to a valuable distribution of economic opportunities.

Affordable housing and gentrification

Gentrification is the process of economic change in a historically disinvested neighborhood, where higher income residents move in and alter the income, education, and racial makeup of the population. Gentrification is a complex urban process that is the consequence of history and economy, but mostly racism.

Racial discrimination along with misguided economic and urban design policies throughout history set the stage for gentrification today. From the 1930s to the 1960s, with a policy known as "redlining," the federal government labeled certain areas unfit for investment to prevent people of color from accessing financing options for homeownership. While this disinvestment was occurring in urban cores, in the same period, the Federal Housing Administration was subsidizing builders that mass-produced suburban housing. This FHA subsidized suburbs had the legal requirement that none of the houses produced were to be sold to African Americans.

Other housing policies of the mid-20th century exacerbated the "white flight" phenomenon from urban cores. As part of this urban exodus, the expansion of the highway system disconnected Black neighborhoods from significant and valuable portions of the city.

The racist and unjust distribution of value in the city was evident once again during the foreclosure crisis of 2008. During the Great Recession, it was unmistakable that communities of color and their neighborhoods were affected disproportionally by subprime lending practices. The combination of financial and urban practices emphasized the lasting effect of the resulting segregated housing. Neighborhoods with a majority of minority population lack economic opportunity, experience increased violence, and have fewer opportunities to access quality education.

Existing zoning barriers emphasize the loss of affordable housing by linking housing types to outdated family and economic models. Even when gentrification is the physical expression of rigid urban planning and racist practices, innovative zoning policies could contribute to a more equitable city. Allowing for heterogeneous housing types in close proximity contributes opportunity to a wider variety of families.

Access to affordable housing affects every aspect of life, from commuting times to personal safety. Unequal access to housing limits economic and educational potential of families and restricts future life opportunities. House values are defined not only by their size and internal features but their surrounding built environment. The emphasis the realtors place when chanting "Location! Location! Location" is the commercial expression on the influence, both negative and positive, that the urban environment provides to daily life, from a tree canopy to the quality of drinking water.

The historic segregation from desirable housing as a means to build wealth remains elusive for racial minorities today. Most affordable housing options are currently available in economically disinvested areas. This unfair approach to urban housing distribution punishes the poor with lower housing quality options and an inadequately served environment.

About NIMBY

Racial discrimination in the city is not just on paper. A long history of dividing the city per zones has reinforced a NIMBY culture. NIMBY is an acronym that stands for "Not In My Back Yard" – it illustrates the opposition of residents to proposed developments in their neighborhood. It is "us" versus "them," it is "go over there" instead of "here." This mindset accentuates the idea that there are zones in the city that should carry the burden of common solutions away from others.

NIMBY has a strong connotation that the resistance to a project is rooted only in the proximity of the project to their own property. From bike lanes to new housing projects, this approach opposes changes to the urban environment that serves a population different from the one already established.

The influence of NIMBY is seen in projects that require integration of urban services, like bicycle lanes. In practice, a healthy network of bike lanes requires continuity throughout the city to be safe and effective. By restricting the implementation of lanes on certain neighborhoods, locals can weaken the whole transportation system that benefits neighbors in other areas. With the same mindset, NIMBY often prevents affordable housing options from being distributed fairly throughout the city by blocking individual projects.

The NIMBY response to residential projects is the louder expression of separating the city by zones. One zone for big houses, one zone for small apartments, one zone for cars, one zone for bicycles. One zone for us, one zone for them. NIMBY wording carries strong racial and discriminatory connotations hidden behind the potential erosion of a historic advantage. From school overcrowding to neighborhood character, the NIMBY arguments are based on the hypothetical negative influence of increasing access to new groups of individuals different from those already established.

NIMBYs oppose new development projects mainly due to lack of trust, the feeling of threat by outsiders, and fear of change. Fueled by digital social networks, distance between neighbors and lack of common understanding of the public space, NIMBYs are politically active and vocal with local media.

Access to housing

Access to affordable housing is not just about putting people in buildings. Affordable housing is closely related to the services residents can access and the capacity of the neighbors to contribute to their own built environment. Unequal distribution of public transportation networks emphasizes the lack of affordable housing options. Convenient access to quality jobs and retail is strongly related to the density and housing options they serve. Transit options and safe pedestrian infrastructure contribute to affordable housing by allowing residents to proactively participate in civic society.

The capacity to maintain quality employment is also closely related to the distance and transit options available for employees. Between 2000 and 2012, residents in high-poverty and majority-minority neighborhoods saw declines in job proximity. The availability to accessible jobs for residents of these neighborhoods dropped at a much faster pace than for the typical suburban resident.

Access to quality shopping is also a factor in housing affordability. Food access is deeply connected to poverty and transportation. Millions of Americans today live in "food deserts." A food desert is a district where the walking distance to a supermarket is more than half a mile, in areas where 40% of households have no car available and the median income is below the poverty level. Proximity and availability to fresh food affects health outcomes of residents in those neighborhoods. Accessible and safe retail options are fundamental to integrate affordable housing into the city.

Available education services are a strong driver to housing affordability. Eviction, foreclosure, and rent increase are associated with higher degrees of school mobility. Students affected by financial challenges are more likely to attend worse performing schools within the same academic year. In fact, frequent moves have a negative impact on education achievement of students. Isolating affordable housing from neighborhoods with better performing schools perpetuates transgenerational poverty.

Affordable housing is only feasible if those neighbors have access to jobs, education, and quality services. The current distribution of houses in the city prevents affordable units from being created where those quality services already exist. Poor people today travel more to work, have less access to fresh food, and are surrounded by fewer educational and healthcare options. Affordable housing is the arena by which each family connects with a supportive social network.

The current housing stock divided by zone only exacerbates the needs of the poor. More housing diversity in larger areas throughout the city may not erase the negative impact of racism in city planning, but the future of housing can create opportunities to reorganize economic prospects for all.

The making of affordable housing

Affordable housing must be accommodating to the evolution of families as they age. A house well designed and built must serve its occupants and allow for alterations that welcome changing needs in the short and long term. Design flexibility anticipates life changes and avoids housing obsolescence.

Far from the typical approach to affordable housing, Alejandro Aravena, the Chilean architect and winner of the 2016 Pritzker Architecture Prize Award, implemented a creative approach to avoid housing obsolescence to affordable housing. When developing social housing designs in Iquique, Chile, he designed a model that could include alterations and additions by each homeowner as future needs may arise for each family. The initial portion of the house included all infrastructure, like bathrooms and kitchens, and allowed for self-completed alterations as the family aged. The original dwelling units were 390 square feet, once all additions were complete, each unit had the capacity to grow up to 750 square feet. This example shows that affordable housing can grow with time based on its occupants' needs and capacity to implement individual changes.

For housing to be affordable it must also be environmentally friendly through reduced energy use, less waste, and better utilization of materials that are long lasting and non-polluting. Through the use of green building materials, appliances and building techniques, sustainable affordable developments benefit low-income residents and contribute to their surrounding communities.

Once considered a luxury, an example of affordable and sustainable housing was designed in New York City, by Dattner Architect and Grimshaw, as a 222-unit affordable housing complex on a reclaimed brownfield site in the Bronx. This project exceeds local environmental standards and reached LEED Gold certification by incorporating a mix of sustainable and affordable living strategies. Photovoltaic solar panels in the roof generate electricity for the building; 34,000 square feet of green roofs offer opportunities for gardening and recreation while reducing storm water run-off and enhancing building insulation.

Along with flexible and sustainable, it is fundamental that affordable housing is financially feasible. Not only must the unit be economically accessible to purchase or rent but it must also be affordable to maintain and operate. Units can be affordable by their compact size but also by sharing spaces and services with others. For example, adding a dwelling unit behind an existing house saves the cost of land and utility connections while also contributing rent income to the homeowner.

Aside from economy and context, affordable housing must be physically accessible to its surrounding environment. For a house to be affordable, it must be convenient to the services its occupants use frequently, like schools, jobs, and healthcare. Access to public transit and pedestrian infrastructure encourages independent living. The concept of accessibility and affordable housing encompasses the capacity of each resident to participate in civic society without the need of a car. Car dependency contributes to the economic burden of those in need of housing while excluding those unable to drive.

I have seen affordable housing alternatives already implemented in the United States. In general, they are far away from much needed services and lack integration to the surrounding environment. They create economic segregated ghettos that separate residents from the rest of the city.

Affordable housing that is integrated to the existing urban network benefits from existing public services, transit options, and infrastructure. Zoning regulations that allow for infill development create opportunities for individuals to thrive in different stages of life, from preschoolers to retirees. Affordable housing distributed throughout the city creates a context that fosters self-agency.

A new paradigm of affordable housing has to comprise the multiple layers of economic and social factors that affords families the ability to thrive in the community they are part of. The outdated idea of affordable housing as a distant option away from established neighborhoods has proved to exacerbate the stigma associated with poverty and lack of opportunities.

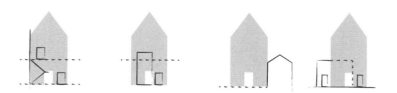

CHAPTER 4

Because Families

When we think about houses, we tend to imagine them as a static box, there and forever. And yet, dwellings have evolved because people who live in them do. But how can a house built in the 1910s still work today? Will the houses built in 2010 still work for the humans of 2110? To understand how housing and families work we must discuss how and where people live.

A large proportion of the housing deficit today is the result of lack of diversity in housing types and sizes. Age, disability, cultural backgrounds, and lifestyle are shapers of home design. How and where we distribute new housing will determine who will have space to thrive.

Aging in place

As people age, the dynamics on how each individual uses the house also shift. Aging in place is associated with accommodating people's needs to the home they have lived in for a long time. There is a strong correlation between age and occupancy of space, because physical and intellectual demands change as we grow older. Features like stairs and bathtubs become inaccessible and harder to use. A widower may not enjoy a large kitchen and dining room that used to host large gatherings in the past. A single person may need more bedrooms after marriage and kids enter the scene. In residential design, age and time matters.

Aging in place fosters independence and strengthens social bonds. To move and change home after each life event is economically unsustainable and socially untenable. The U.S. Department of Housing has found evidence that programs that support the elderly to age in place yields cost savings for families, government, and healthcare systems. Even when costs of care vary greatly in each individual case, the emotional attachment to a known social and physical environment fosters self-agency.

Existing housing stock for elders and people with disabilities makes aging in place challenging. Large homes distributed in multiple levels separate daily life activities, like the cooking and bathing, with flights of stairs. The internal barriers of aging in places are compounded by low-density zones that exacerbate car dependency as the main mode of transportation, and reduce opportunities to an active social life. The lack of safe pedestrian infrastructure and distance from essential services create physical barriers to connect with others. The existing stock of housing has interior layouts in an environment that is an obstacle to age in place.

The design of homes and their surrounding neighborhood is fundamental to foster independence in all stages of life. Aging in place is the ability to live in one's own home and community welcomed by spaces that promote safety, independence, and comfort, regardless of age, income, or ability level.

Because aging in place is so beneficial from an individual and social perspective, a series of measures can contribute to a safer and stimulating built environment. Universal design provides opportunities to equitable and flexible use of space and objects. This design approach results in a simple and intuitive way to engage with objects, and requires low physical effort to enjoy. Universal design, as a complement to accessible design, produces buildings that are aesthetically pleasing and usable to the greatest extent possible by everyone regardless of age, status in life, and physical ability. Examples of this can be seen in building access through ramps, door widths, and even pill bottles. Universal design promotes social integration through comprehensive use of a shared environment, private and public.

Until recently, aging in place focused on late life stages, and yet there is a constant evolution of the use of space. Aging, after all, is a continuum in family life. After opening my architecture firm, I noticed that most of my clients required design services after a significant life event: weddings and divorces, new parents and empty nesters, blended families, and every other family format in between. When exploring design ideas to satisfy family needs, I noticed a pattern in changes of family aging: expansion, contraction, and stability.

The transition between life stages re-establishes the dynamics on how the new family occupies space. As families age, their spatial dynamic – private and public – also shifts.

Families and home

It is natural to think that families only grow with the addition of children. Most houses in the market today assume that parents with small children will occupy the building… forever. In my experience, many of the design projects we are engaged with involve families that grow and evolve in alternative ways. Many of our clients decide to welcome an older generation into the property; others require space for children with special needs that require semi-independent facilities. Because the nuclear family is more fluid than in the past, there is also no model home that can satisfy the variety of housing demand today.

A family grows when more individuals occupy the home full time. Naturally seen as a need for just additional bedrooms, the growth of a family is also a balance to share individual and common spaces: bedrooms versus family rooms. Depending on the size of the family and the age of its members, privacy, support, and services are organizers on how each individual can contribute to the dynamic of a shared property. Couples with small children occupy the home differently from couples with adult children.

But families change not only by growing; children age and leave the nest, and couples break up. Oversized and under-occupied housing is expensive and unsustainable. Excess space has the potential to transform interior uses and contribute to quality of life. Existing excess space can be transformative as a financial contributor as well. An unused basement can become a separate apartment. An oversized garage can be converted into a granny flat.

Aside from families changing in size, other units are stable through decades. A family size is stable when the perspective of space needs occupancy is fixed in the long term. Families made up of adults only and single people rarely change space needs based on size, but their use of space is mostly influenced by age, physical ability, and economic conditions. These households can plan for the long term of the building based on personal choices.

The idea of moving every time the family size and dynamics change is unsustainable economically and socially. Different from moving at each life stage, innovative home design and occupancy welcomes age as the potential to thrive in a familiar environment.

The urban and social bonds of aging in place cannot be oversimplified. Staying home during multiple stages of life strengthens neighborhood bonds, fosters community, and contributes to a local economy through shopping, education, and culture. Neighbors that know each other can be of crucial assistance in moments of crisis. Aging in place is feasible when the conditions of private property and the quality of the public space support neighbors' physical and intellectual needs.

The desire to stay home through family stages, from parenthood to retirement, has a direct building and zoning expression. Residential design and urban planning have had a strong influence on how a home is shaped. Even as the concept of family has evolved through history, cities today overregulate how a home can be occupied. The overreliance of zones dedicated to single-family homes limits the possibility to age in place and excludes new models of nuclear families.

But what is a family today? What constitutes a single-family home, then?

Families: A brief history

Early in American history, a family consisted of a married couple with biological children and extended family, except in the case of slaves. This dominant familial structure emphasized the roles of each member, and their financial contribution to the unit.

The 19th century brought property rights to women along with rights for children such as school attendance and labor restrictions. During this period, the family transformed from an economic unit to an emotional one. The idea of family became one based on love, companionship, and choice. In fact, divorce rates tripled in the period from 1860 to 1910 and became a new sign of the evolution of marriages and family model in America.

A more dynamic model of household took shape early in the 20th century when economic participation increased for each family member during the Great Depression. Even if traditional roles prevailed during the 1930s, the lack of work for males forced women and children to seek low-paying employment options outside the home. Marriage rates declined along with decreased birth rates, and multiple families crowded homes designed as single-family residences.

The post-World War II period was fundamental in shaping the concept of family unit we still have today. Despite the nuclear family depicted in television shows of the time, the reality was that only 60% of children spent their childhood in households made up of a male breadwinner and female homemaker. This disconnection between the ideal picture family and the reality remained for decades.

The economic boom of the 1950s resulted in 13 million new homes being built, mostly in the suburbs. The idea of escaping urban brutality was born then and it cemented the pastoral view of American domesticity. Family, home, and the romanticized view of the suburbs became the ideal standard of life. The idea of a protected, economically stable and safe home in the 1950s was anchored in the notion of protecting one's own from others.

A significant shift in nuclear family models appeared in the 1960s. Starting in this period, families become smaller, less stable, and more diverse. Middle-class women increased their participation in the workforce, and adults – young and old – lived outside the family unit. Two-earner families became the new norm. The number of unmarried and childless individuals increased at a greater rate than any other time before in history.

Today, more than 50% of households are headed by an unmarried person, and half of paid labor is made up by women. Increased legal protections for marriages and divorce expand the diversity of married couples, such as race and gender composition. Even if about 90% of Americans do marry today, their marriages look different, are formed at different times, and dissolve at a different pace than in the past.

Households with children under 18 in the United States make up 40% of all homes. Of those, about half were headed by single mothers and one third was made up of married couples. Of all the households in the United States in 1960, one-person households were just 13%, in 2020 this number jumped to 28%. The estimated average age when people marry increased from 23 in 1947 to 30 years old in 2020. Even if these statistics from the U.S. Census Bureau were taken before the 2020 pandemic, they are still representative of the household composition of the American family.

The fluctuation of family models in recent decades illustrates how the homogeneous approach to housing models provides a disservice to the current American family unit. The current housing stock remains stubborn in housing a type of family that started fading more than half a century ago. New social and economic realities demand dynamism in the approach to residential design and zoning regulations.

What is a single-family home?

A single-family home is defined as a stand-alone residential structure that is maintained and used by a single owner. These types of buildings are detached from others and surrounded by a yard. Single family homes are the most common housing type in the country, in fact, about 82% of Americans live in them.. This housing type, the most prevalent in America, means that one house equals one nuclear family. The predominance of this housing type has not evolved to reflect social and economic changes. Single-family homes are associated with certain aesthetic, distance from others, and most importantly, the use of cars as the main mode of transportation.

Raised in Argentina, as a child of the 1980s, I grew up watching Hollywood movies. In the background of all the outdoor scenes you could see a large front yard, a driveway – with a basketball hoop! – and plenty of space between neighbors. Thirty years later, when working with my own clients' projects I discovered how ill-fitting the cultural export of house models was. From Home Alone to Edward Scissorhands, as an architect I wonder about what is considered normal housing. As an adult living in America now, I wonder about the complexity of racial, economic, and cultural significance of the fictional idea of home and family. What if there is not a typical family home?

The idea of one family per house is new. In preindustrial times, most people lived in multifamily dwellings for most of their lives. Living with their parents, children remained in the household until marriage. The idea of the nuclear family living separately from their relatives is a recent development in the American and European modern eras. Plentiful land in the Americas reinforced the idea of privacy and space and it was fueled by car ownership.

The idea of suburban housing as the ideal model to raise a family and create wealth was cemented in the 1950s and continues today. The ownership of homes with a yard surrounded by a "white picket fence" has been seen as a fundamental part of the American Dream since then. However, racist financial and housing practices have decreased the opportunities to build wealth through homeownership for minorities.

The outdoor space: private and public

Housing typology is closely related to the availability of indoor and outdoor spaces. Additional dwelling units, as a housing option for existing low-density areas, contribute a design opportunity to increase the use of outdoor space, from private to public.

From parking to play pens, landscaping and granny flats, demand for outdoor space evolves as a family ages. Households with children benefit from access to a secured outdoor space that allows for unsupervised activities. However, as each member grows older, maintenance efforts and costs associated with landscaping are burdensome. Residential outdoor spaces have the capacity to incorporate features, structures and elements that promote independent living for people of all ages: from a swing set to raised gardening beds. Dedicated outdoor space for parking can transform from a patio for entertainment to a charging station for an electric car. The use of outdoor space evolves with the needs of families throughout time, making room for those changes allows for houses to be more accommodating to its residents as they age.

Age is also a factor in the type and intensity of infrastructure usage: the quality of public transit, bicycle lanes, and sidewalks emphasize the relationship between individuals and their surrounding community. The potential for frequent use of the public domain contributes to a sense of belonging.

The pandemic of 2020 accelerated changes in work and education along with an intensity of the use of public space. The impact of this historic health crisis re-established the relationship between citizens and the significance of public space as a support network to the home. From retail to offices and schools, Covid-19 reshaped the connections between private spaces and the surrounding community through the built environment.

Shut out from my office, and my children learning from home, our afternoons were filled with walks around the neighborhood in search of a break from routine. We observed how small businesses, with the support of local municipalities, opened up to the new economic reality.

This collaboration between government and businesses transformed parking lanes into street-eateries, allowed for sidewalk shopping, and built a new environment that welcomed pedestrians. As I write this book, the impact of coronavirus in the long-term planning of the city is hard to predict, but I cherish the spaces created with ingenuity and creativity. This intensification of the use of home for work also has impact on opportunities to create a wider variety of retail options within walking distance of residential neighborhoods.

The reduced demand for public transportation and an increase of walking and biking became the transit revelation of the health crisis of 2020. The commute of the future has the potential to become more flexible and open to innovative modes of transportation. However, housing types and interior layouts must accommodate features that facilitate the use of alternative transit options. Better interior design, such as convenient bicycle parking and storage, can contribute to less frequent use of cars. Patios can also become electric charging stations fueled by photovoltaic panels. In the public realm, the safety of bike paths, and availability of bicycle parking at each destination, reinforces the use of alternative transportation for people of all ages and abilities.

Improved transportation options will also depend on the type of housing that is available in each neighborhood. The implementation of denser and alternative housing types organizes the use of the public space in the future. From granny flats to basement apartments, new housing models contribute density and strengthen connectivity. Small design gestures, from bicycle parking to a shaded bench, create a welcoming physical environment that normalizes the use of transit. Accessible infrastructure inside and outside the home is the key to reduce car usage without interfering with daily life. Compared to the car keys, how accessible is your bicycle now?

Shared economy: from housing to music

Along with family and housing formats, new generations are reshaping the idea of transportation. Fueled by environmental concerns, the millennial generation embraces car access over car ownership. Even when historically considered a rite of passage for many Americans, today 55% of adults aged 18 to 34 make an effort to drive less. Buoyed by programs of the shared economy, the new generations participate in sharing of tangible items, like homes and vacation options, along with intangible goods, such as music and movies. This mode of collaborative consumption is not only reshaping car ownership but also the idea of housing.

The current collaborative consumption of goods, from videogames to cars, illustrates how future generations will embrace housing models. This intangible value in ownership reshapes the level of acceptable shared benefits. This economic model of detaching a benefit from the physical environment has rewritten the idea of space. Future generations will continue to spend money on goods and services that do not take physical space.

In this format, sharing a backyard with a granny flat is more acceptable for a younger generation used to sharing music and movies with peers. Denser and more innovative housing layouts will become the norm as younger generations enter the market as homeowners.

Independent living by design

I learned one of the most important kitchen design lessons by observing my own family. As my own kids aged, from toddlerhood into small-kid size, their capacity to cooperate with chores also grew. Aside from self-care tasks, like brushing their teeth or picking up toys – after a LOT of begging – I noticed that they were able to perform simple helping tasks as they aged.

However, their capacity to get water, grab plastic flatware, and reach for paper towels to clean up (a little bit) after themselves was heavily conditioned by their surrounding environment. The height of cabinets, the type of storage, and the availability of space limited their capacity to perform age-appropriate tasks. Their intellectual and physical ability to help was limited by their size. None of the lower cabinets in the kitchen had been designed to store items that a child could use to manage independently. All the lower cabinets were hollow giant boxes where heavy pots and pans went, more useful to play hide-and-seek than to helping with kitchen chores. Plates and cups were in upper cabinets, too high and dangerous for my children to reach. This example illustrates how the design and location of each element of the home limits the capacity for each individual of the household to contribute to their own needs, no matter the age and physical ability.

On the opposite end of the age spectrum, an older individual may see her capacity to perform tasks independently limited by the distribution of uses around the house. Navigating multiple flights of stairs with a laundry basket or climbing ladders to reach upper cabinets are a reflection of the demands of space to adapt to age and physical ability.

These built-in constraints for independent living are not limited to the interior spaces. The connections between public and private space for people of all ages requires a change in the mindset of home. The current stock of single-family homes in low-density neighborhoods creates a series of invisible barriers that have become culturally acceptable but shouldn't be. From car dependency to lack of transit options, new housing models have the capacity to contribute to independent living within and outside the house.

Alternative housing types, like backyard cottages, welcome not only older generations to the urban core but also increased autonomous participation for children. In this new housing model, the shared backyard becomes a new layer of connectivity for those requiring independent and safe living conditions.

Self-sufficiency within the home is strongly associated to design details, such as kitchen cabinets, but also how each house relates to others in the neighborhood. A home with safe places for children and the elderly to interact fosters

•

autonomy. A small child can visit a grandparent when the distance that separates them is the length of the backyard, and reduces car dependency for intergenerational activities.

Institutionalized housing

Housing options for the non-typical family remain scarce. The pandemic of 2020 has highlighted the shortage of housing options for the elderly and for those living with disabilities. Institutionalized and large-scale facilities for those groups was the context where that population suffered from a disproportionate impact of Covid-19 in number of cases and deaths. The spread of the coronavirus was harder to contain and more deadly as the building typology was more homogeneous: from assisted living facilities to jails.

The lack of housing options for the elderly has multiple causes, from health to economic. Assisted living facilities became popular as part of the suburbanization of America in the post-war period but did not become ubiquitous until the 1965 enactment of Medicare and Medicaid. Lack of oversight and a dispersion in standards of care resulted in the enormous impact of Covid-19 on its population. Grouped housing along with age vulnerabilities affected this population on a larger scale than any other social and age groups. In fact, early research shows that families are re-evaluating that traditional housing format for their older family members.

The health and emotional experience of the pandemic of 2020 will reshape how Americans will care for the elderly in the future. Covid-19 has caused more than 115,000 deaths linked to U.S. long-term care institutions.

Even when a proportion of the population benefits from shared and highly specialized care services located in one building, a wider variety of housing options has the capacity to provide shelter. The lack of affordable housing options emphasizes the demand for new housing typologies dedicated to individuals capable of living independently. The current format of large institutional housing as one of the few options for aging limits the options of each individual to contribute to their own wellbeing.

I have seen the demand of housing for individuals with disabilities in my own studio when a client reached out to create an additional dwelling unit behind her townhouse. The future resident of the project, a relative with special needs, can live independently under supervision, but none of the existing housing options in the market satisfied her needs. The client and her family realized that an apartment in the backyard had the capacity to provide housing with the family support she needed. Located within an established neighborhood with proximity to retail and services, the new unit offers opportunities for her participation in civic society.

Proximity to existing shopping options, healthcare services and education makes infill housing a good alternative for individuals of all ages and intellectual abilities. Vicinity to family members contributes potential for assistance in times of need while reducing car dependency. Innovative housing formats within the existing urban context promote new ways for individuals and families to strengthen their support network.

Age and isolation

Housing layout and design organizes family life. From holidays to snow days, barbecues, and birthdays, how we experience the private space with others contributes to our identity as citizens. Shared levels of privacy contribute to quality of life and cultural enrichment. Lack of connection with others and social isolation are twice as harmful to physical and mental health as obesity. The most recent U.S. census data shows that more than a quarter of the population lives alone, the highest ever recorded. Aside from housing models, the participation in religion and volunteerism has also declined, reducing community connection with the surrounding environment. Connection with others is a human need.

But what is isolation? Chronic loneliness is experienced by individuals who lack the emotional, mental, or financial resources to nurture their social needs. The lack of supportive social circles emphasizes the negative impact of isolation. Frequent loneliness is associated with a weak social and community life accentuated by functional limitations, disability, and low levels of family assistance.

This way, the construction of houses that strengthen social supportive networks within existing neighborhoods can be a framework for vulnerable populations. The intentional habitation of a shared property, from a main house to a granny flat, strengthens the network of care and increases the potential for collaboration. From landscape to fences, from views and access, the location and layout of additional dwelling units can contribute to the relationship between homeowner and tenant.

Occupants of the same property can share hobbies in the common spaces, like gardening or outdoor cooking. Residents of different cultures can share religious ceremonies in common spaces, from Christmas to Diwali. Proximity of people different from each other can break cultural and linguistic barriers. Residents of different age groups can find cooperation in shared chores, from grocery shopping to childcare. The negative effects of social isolation can be reduced by physical proximity of new housing models within the existing urban context.

Multigenerational housing

If the idea of nuclear family is so fluid, why are our houses still designed the way they are? One in five Americans lives in a multigenerational household. The number increased from 42 million in 2000 to 64 million in 2016. Multigenerational families are those consisting of more than two generations living under the same roof. This jump in shared households saw a sharp uptick during and immediately after the Great Recession of 2008. Based on census data, multigenerational households are growing among nearly all racial groups and genders. In fact, millennials living with parents – young adults between 18 to 34 – surpassed other living arrangements for the first time in more than a century.

Choosing to merge multiple generations under one roof carries several layers of challenges and benefits. Advantages can be seen in reduced living expenses and shared housing responsibilities. Younger members of the family can carry the physical burden of maintenance and repairs while extended families living in close proximity enjoy intergenerational supervisory care. This arrangement reduces cost of living and adds convenience to each generation of the household.

From a cultural point of view, multigenerational living develops stronger ethnic bonds with older members of the family. Unstructured shared time allows for transfer of language and family culture between generations, from food to language. This living arrangement also reduces loneliness and allows older members to stay active and engaged. Younger adults receive support that lessens the stresses of daily life, from cooking to childcare. Multigenerational households benefit children particularly if only one parent lives in the household.

Multigenerational households have a strong correlation to culture and origin; the growing racial and ethnic diversity in the United States carries a larger representation in this type of arrangement. Asian and Hispanic populations are more likely than whites to live in multigenerational households. Also, foreign born Americans are more likely than those born in the country to share their household with extended family. Among Asians living in the United States in 2016, 29% lived in multigenerational housing while Hispanics and Blacks represented 27%. Multigenerational housing was 16% for whites.

The association between house and family is so strong in some cultures that in Hawaiian, the word "ohana" is used to mean both family and home. The word encompasses extended family, not just those related by blood but also adoptive members and intentional bonds. Additional dwelling units in Hawaii are called "ohana unit" and it means both the house and the family living in the same property.

Design for age, early steps

To design homes is also to design for change. Once becoming a mom, 20 years after I graduated from architecture school, I observed how my own children occupied and organized the space that surrounded them. This observation has enriched the academic design lessons learned two decades before. Formed around a mix of architecture, interior design, and furniture, the growth of a child illustrates the dynamic evolution of age and physical ability at all life stages. An efficient and effective residential design accommodates for the impact of aging in the built environment. By understanding how each person occupies their own space, conscious residential design can introduce flexibility for all ages and stages of life.

So how do we design with children? Within the home, before the age of one, babies share the same physical space as the adults that care for them. All elements that encourage and support this closeness appear in the house and take up a lot of space, from cribs to tubs and storage for diapers. That physical intimacy between family members can be seen in Baby Björns and carriers as promoters of some level of physical freedom for the adult while keeping physical closeness with the child. Because all activities are adult-dependent, sleeping, eating, and bathing are performed in shared spaces between adults and small children. Before the first year, the family benefits from interior spaces that accommodates multiple people for shared tasks.

There is a significant change in the use of interior residential space between the ages of one and two. The physical distance between adults and children grows and children occupy floor space in the same room where the parents are. The living room becomes a play pen, stairs are fitted with gates to prevent unsafe climbing, and yes, toys are everywhere. The habit of sleeping in separate rooms becomes feasible and even desirable. Even if adult and child perform tasks separately, like cooking and playing, visual connections are essential to ensure safety. Open floor layouts are beneficial for this stage in the child's life where visibility contributes to safety but also fosters independence.

Between the ages of two and four, I was excited to discover that my kids were comfortable occupying a room not visually connected to me. I could be folding laundry in one room and they could be playing in the room next door. Even if this separation did not offer any privacy, these few steps of separation built a small range of autonomy. Adjacent rooms with open doors allowed for visual privacy and provided security and closeness.

After my kids turned four years old, there was a significant change in the use of space. After this age, they gained independence in navigating the house vertically and horizontally. From the basement to the second floor, the house became a series of spaces to be explored independently from me. The physical distance between parents and children influenced age-appropriate privacy, from naptime to playtime.

This fast-paced change in the use of space for children illustrates how physical and intellectual capabilities condition the occupancy of the home. As people age, we see how the desire for privacy, independence and self-reliance also evolves significantly. This process is meaningful from early childhood to the teenage years, but it does not stop there. Boomerang children, older adults, and blended families all use the space based on needs of autonomy, safety, and need for socialization in the household. Room sizing and distribution around the house contributes to the impact of aging at home, from early years to adulthood. Innovative residential design can create housing models that provide shelter for a wider range of age that is representative of current family formats.

Distribution and connections with age

Space distribution within the home, its infrastructure, and quality of space should promote the reusing of space as the family ages. Pacifiers, keys, and laundry baskets must travel between floors along with those who use them. The organization of spaces within each level and between levels evolves significantly as the occupants age. The flexibility of each room to accommodate different pieces of furniture as the family ages allows the ground floor toy room to become an office, and even a bedroom for those who cannot navigate stairs at night. The size of each room, its location in the house, and connections to services like bathrooms and kitchen, contributes to independent living in the long term.

The evolution in the use of interior space as a person ages is also a reflection on how they relate to the urban environment. Newborns cannot use the public space autonomously in the same way they are not able to use interior space independently from adults. Younger children, however, can play on the porch, or share the sidewalk with a neighbor to ride a bike. As children age, their capacity to occupy public spaces safely is dependent on the surrounding physical environment, from the design of sidewalks to parks.

Additional dwelling units provide a new level of private and public safety within the housing stock. Granny flats enrich private yards as safe connectors between children and adults. Additional entrances along the sidewalk to access basement apartments contribute activity to the streetscape. Innovative housing that increases density enriches the public realm by adding intensity of use.

Also, boomerang children

A new phenomenon in residential design and multigenerational housing is the shared space with blood-related young adults. The empty-nesters of the past have turned into full-nesters once again. Known as boomerang children, members of this generation are participants of a trend of young adults returning to live with their parents for economic reasons after a period of independent living. By 2016, about 15% of millennials lived in their parents' home.

By mid-2020 with the impact of the Covid-19 pandemic, 52% of young adults returned home to live with their parents. Financial reasons, low wages, low savings, high student debt, and lack of social welfare networks are some of the causes of young working adults returning to live with their parents. The long-term consequences of the economic impact of the pandemic of 2020 will be seen in upcoming decades when data shows the housing impact of work from home mandates.

The traditional format of single-family homes in low-density neighborhoods is a poor contributor of housing format for related adults to live together after a period of independent living. Different from bedrooms clustered together, separate dwellings within the property provide flexible space for boomerang children in need of private and independent affordable options. This housing format operates autonomously from the main house at a much lower cost to the parents than the cost of two separate households.

Despite the need of affordable housing across cultures and family realities, most zoning regulations today limit the number of dwelling units allowable per lot. This restricts the potential for properties to extend private living arrangements to different members of the family as needs arise. It is expected that future planning efforts will organize the potential growth for multifamily housing based on the proximity to transit, massing models, and demand for multigenerational households.

A network of care and the sandwich generation

When it comes to housing typology, it is relevant to remember how the location, size, and cost of home affects each member of society. The sandwich generation is made up of a new group of people, mostly women, pressured with opposing social demands. Burdened by an aging population and a generation of young adults that lack financial independence, middle-aged Americans are encumbered with care for both groups.

Almost half of adults today in the United States in their 40s and 50s have a parent aged 65 or older, and are raising a child at the same time. One in seven middle-aged adults also provides financial support to both aging parents and children. Even if the share of middle-aged adults living in this sandwich generation has marginally increased in recent years, the financial burdens associated with caring for multiple generations are escalating.

From career to family, the sandwich generation plans and performs care for younger and older people, and one of the most important ingredients in this stressed-out social group is how and where people live. The current division of housing type based on age heavily conditions how much each individual can provide and receive care tied to their ability to drive.

Senior living communities are the most popular option for retirees today. Housing for the elderly is organized by the level of care that each institution provides. From assisted living facilities to gated communities for those aged 55 and over. The common thread of this housing type for elders is the distance from traditional neighborhoods occupied by other age groups.

Grouping retirement communities outside the city creates an additional barrier in the integration to organized activities with other social groups. If new housing types within the urban network allowed for affordable and accessible units, the participation of senior citizens to larger society can increase. Institutionalized housing emphasizes a car-dependent culture that adds stress to family members, increases cost for caretakers, and reduces community participation.

There is a strong correlation between the stress of caring for others and the accessibility of that support. The demands to plan, tend to, and be alert to a crisis result in an unmanageable schedule of doctors' appointments, emergency room visits, and planned family events. Coordination and transport alone make older members less likely to be contributors to their own self-care.

The capacity and willingness to drive is independent from the ability to care for others. Children could walk to grandma's if she were to live in a house in the backyard.

Teenagers can contribute tech support and run errands for the older generation. Additional dwelling units, their location, and connections to the main house, contribute to individual self-agency, no matter the age of the resident. These smaller units, sharing the yard with the main house, add to housing for nannies, grandparents, and even single-parent families looking for household support. Additional dwelling units create buildings that strengthen a supportive social network.

From teachers to dog walkers, nurses, and retirees, allowing affordable housing within the existing neighborhoods reduces how care and services are delivered to those who need it most. Before additional dwelling units became an urban trend, my own sister was an example on how this housing format created support between residents. When Guillermina attended graduate school in California, she rented the basement of a house in Monterrey. Part of the rent was afforded by caring for the family's six-year-old child. Her role as a caretaker included school support, playtime, and occasional nanny care for the parents' night out. The relationship between the homeowners and my sister was the result of a service exchange that reduced the cost of rent. The housing type also allowed for a new type of relationship between homeowner and renter that provided financial and social benefits to both parties. The housing format, and the closeness to the family that owned the home, also contributed to a positive introduction to the American culture.

The convenience of innovative housing

Frequent care for others and the time it takes to travel between obligations contributes to stress and cost. Daily commutes, school and after-school activities, dentists' appointments, and soccer practice must all fit between breakfast and dinner, or even during those times. Since public transit is not always available where activities happen, a car-dependent caretaker must travel between events: children to soccer practice, elderly parents to check-ups, and so on.

The benefits of additional dwelling units for caretakers are illustrated by the daily time demands, such as the transition between school and home. The new housing model generates income and social bonds for the caretakers while allowing flexibility for the parents. This relationship of assistance strengthens social engagement through part-time intergenerational collaboration. Even if the person in charge is not capable of driving or does not want to own a car at all, the closeness of the housing units allows for that service to be feasible for all.

For example, creating an accessible dwelling unit off of a renovated garage can provide barrier-free housing for an older adult. Even if this person were to need physical support to shovel snow, or other able-bodied demanding activities, she has the capacity to be in charge of drop-off and pick-up of the neighborhood's kid at school. Individual self-sufficiency is heavily conditioned by the environment where each individual lives and the capacity to contribute to the greater good. With this new housing format, giving up a car does not mean isolation. In fact, the proximity of housing to school and other services provides opportunity to support younger generations by walking and transit.

Housing isolation exacerbates social isolation. Homogeneous housing distribution in the city exacerbates differences in how each social group can contribute to larger society. Additional dwelling units within the existing housing stock create the space for those currently excluded from the city to regain a footing in the social and urban network everyone can benefit from.

The impact of car dependency

The benefits of walking to and from daily activities have been shown in multiple health studies. Building physical activity into a routine increases fitness and reduces risk of heart disease. Walking to school, work, and shopping contributes easy options to exercise recommended by doctors. And yet, for walking to be feasible, the built environment must provide design conditions for everyone. Sidewalks, street lighting, and safe traffic intersections are some of the elements that contribute and stimulate pedestrian mobility as a part of daily life.

Walkability is a measure of how friendly an area is to walking and it is measured by evaluating the amount and types of services within a mile of a home. Factors that contribute to walkability include footpaths, sidewalks, and pedestrians' rights-of-way. Walkability is such a factor in quality of life that it even affects property values.

Continuity of pedestrian paths creates a healthy physical environment that promotes socioeconomic benefits. Foot traffic increases sales in locally owned shops, employers attract staff to jobs that are within walking distance to housing options. Walkability also encourages routine contact with neighbors, increases a sense of belonging, and improves city participation. The strongest social network in the city is the communal public space that everyone can share: the sidewalk.

Housing density and continuity of the streetscape are the main contributors to a pedestrian-friendly environment. Car-dependent communities add tangible and intangible burdens to society. From an individual's perspective, a car comes with costs associated to purchase, operation, and maintenance, along with the space to park it at home. Car dependency also has public costs associated to environmental impacts, unsafe conditions for non-drivers, and infrastructure costs. External impact of car dependency also affects areas where the cars are not even present, by increasing air pollution, contributing to climate change, and soil pollution. Excessive automobile reliance reduces economic productivity and potential for development. A balanced approach to urban transit options contributes to an equitable access to housing and services.

Housing availability, design, and distribution within the city is fundamental to understand how innovative models can make it easier to care for others. Decoupling the concept of home, age, and car allows for each member of society to contribute to the common good based on their physical and intellectual abilities. The current segregation of housing is unsustainable for future generations.

CHAPTER 5

How Houses Adapt and Evolve

Cities are not static open-air museums; their shape and size evolve with time. Because populations grow, it is relevant to understand how cities can and must adapt to an ever-increasing pressure in housing demand and rising cost of urban living. Healthy cities change to accommodate economic and cultural realities of their inhabitants. Cities, like forests, must grow to survive. But how that growth happens makes the difference to which individuals will find a home to thrive.

City planning must anticipate future space needs while addressing the current housing crisis. Sustainable growth of cities must support populations with education, jobs, and infrastructure while providing intensity of use and addressing cultural changes of its population.

How cities grow

There are different formats on how cities grow in size. The typical historic pattern of urban growth followed a concentric circle around denser areas. The city expanded around a central hub of economic activity where the most valuable properties were located. The closer each property was to the core, the higher its value. Large urban areas like New York and Chicago followed this pattern of growth early in their history.

Transit infrastructure affected urban growth patterns in the modern era. Through transportation hubs, cities grew in axial patterns following the implementation of train stations and other methods of mass transit. The effective movement of people and goods to and from the city center expanded the radius of what was considered urban areas. Residential and commercial projects developed along those transportation lines resulted in increased property values on each transit hub.

The distribution of neighborhoods and suburbs in Washington, DC is an example of this type of axial urban growth. A network of horsecar trolleys started operating in 1862 with horsecars and were transformed to electric in 1901; the development of middle-class residential neighborhoods followed these lines that extended well into Virginia and Maryland. This above-ground system was finally dismantled in 1960. Bus lines and the subway partially replaced the historic above-ground lines but essentially continue to emphasize urban growth in an axial pattern.

Different from concentric or axial, sector growth is the pattern of urban expansion that follows individual developments. It is a combination of the axial pattern along with specific magnet projects. The growth happens outward from the city and concentrates uses by type. American development of zoned maps follows this pattern of growth, by type of use and shape of buildings. University campuses create sector growth by concentrating new uses, like higher education, and attracting students, professors, and staff to a clustered area. Demand of services and housing increases in sectors of the city heavily influenced by long-term and large developments.

American cities have followed a combination of growth patterns listed above. However, recently, there has been a reversal on urban growth. Historically cities grew outward buoyed by affordable land and accessible highways. In recent years, distant suburban developments burdened families with long commutes and the social cost of car dependency. The current market demands smaller homes near activity centers that result in new projects in more convenient locations to daily activities.

Innovative urban housing and production

Cities do not grow in an abstract manner. Their expansion materializes in the addition of buildings, infrastructure, and increased demand for services. So how does new housing happen?

Traditionally, new housing occurred as new buildings in empty land. A private developer would purchase undeveloped land on the outskirts of the city, normally the suburbs, and build single-family homes. Supported by highways, shopping malls, and the suburbanization of services, this type of housing development increased distances and emphasized a car-dependent culture. The units developed maximized size and value while creating homogeneous results of single-family homes. It is cheaper to plan, build, and finance than heterogeneous housing. This development of housing growth excludes affordable units and limits the models of houses available for purchase. Because land near urban centers is becoming scarce, the availability of acreage to continue this type of housing growth is unsustainable from a social and economic perspective.

Aside from suburban and exurban growth, urban residential growth also happens with the replacement of existing units. In these areas, developers buy outdated older homes, demolish them, and build a new one from scratch. The tangible consequence of this type of project is the replacement of a smaller, affordable unit with a larger, more expensive one. The cost of buying a home in the same lot increases and the availability of new affordable housing is reduced. Current zoning and financial models encourage the replacement of single-family housing but discourage the conversion into multiple units on the same lot.

Aside from replacement of individual homes, new housing units are created through large-scale multistory projects. Due to the impact on established neighborhoods, this type of project requires coordination between city and developers. They tend to be located in high traffic corridors and result in the densification of a small area. Existing neighbors have little to no influence in the remediation measures that a high-impact project will have. The main benefit of large-scale residential projects is the potential to revitalize disinvested areas providing density to retail and services options on the ground floor, like a grocery store or a day care center.

Aside from large-scale projects, another contributor of new housing can be found in the addition of middle-height housing projects. These types of developments, up to four stories, introduce middle density to neighborhoods. The visual and environmental impact of these projects is limited to the existing streetscape and contributes small-scale retail space on the ground floor, like restaurants and cafes.

An example of this type of middle-scale project can be seen in Petworth, a neighborhood in north-west Washington, DC. The main roads that traverse the neighborhood are converting existing townhouses while providing infill units. The new projects blend with the neighboring structures and allow for existing housing units to be preserved in the surrounding smaller streets. These types of projects are contributors to the local economy by providing ground floor commercial space to small business owners.

Aside from multiunit residential projects, an innovative option to add new housing in the city is the creation of units within existing homes. Located in backyards, basements, and attics, these types of units do not require public participation and have little to no impact on the streetscape. Additional dwelling units contribute one or two extra units per lot by optimizing the use of land in low-density neighborhoods. They illustrate a private solution to the public housing deficit. The aesthetic impact of these types of housing is negligible to the urban environment. They do not provide retail fronts, but the spaces open the possibility for small businesses such as professional services to grow within residential neighborhoods. Detached accessory structures are ideal to use as a dwelling, an office, and small industries like a bicycle repair shop.

The creation of new housing types to satisfy the current housing deficit is dependent on the urban impact, the involvement of parties, and the capacity of each entity to contribute a local solution. The typology of units, the availability of services, and the relationship between private and public space is fundamental for the city to provide sustainable housing options in the long term.

How buildings grow

Just like cities expand with patterns, the buildings that constitute the city can also grow and change through time. Buildings make up urban density and intensity. A diversity of uses, like retail and offices, contribute intensity, meanwhile larger buildings contribute density. The growth of a building can happen horizontally, vertically, and by incorporating new structures on the property.

When growing a house upward, the building replaces its existing roof with additional habitable area. Typical in tight urban settings, this type of growth contributes private spaces, such as bedrooms and bathrooms. Even if this type of addition does not affect the footprint of the house, it does affect its presence on the street. A drawback of adding area to the top of a house is the need of vertical circulation, such as stairs and corridors, which makes each level less efficient.

But a house can also grow downward, by incorporating the use of its basement as habitable space. A house can gain useable area by adding the lowest level of the house into common and support spaces, such as family room and laundry. Depending on site conditions and property values, incorporating the basement as living space becomes a desirable residential investment.

In fact, my first experience with a residential renovation was the addition of a basement to a 1913 townhouse in the Eckington neighborhood of Washington, DC. Our own family home! The house, the typical DC rowhouse, was distributed in three levels but only the ground floor and second were habitable. Traditionally used for storage and mechanical systems, we decided to incorporate the basement by underpinning the foundations and creating a comfortable ceiling height with as much natural light as possible.

Before the project started, the house felt tight for three people and our dog, a wheaten terrier named Cecilia. Because of the small footprint of the house and its tiny backyard – I once bought an umbrella that went over the neighbor's property! – our only option to grow was to incorporate the basement as living space. After a few sketches – well, more than a few, considering my husband is also an architect – we decided that the basement would be excavated to incorporate a family room, bathroom, and workshop. A year after the project was complete, my own architecture firm started in a corner of that basement, a decade before working from home became the norm.

Aside from upward and downward, a house can also grow horizontally. By replacing sections of the exterior walls, this type of growth toward the rear and sides allows for a mix of spaces, private and common, distributed at each level. This type of growth is feasible in lower density neighborhoods where freestanding structures and distance from lot lines allow for occupying more land. A rear addition has the potential to contribute a variety of interior spaces; an additional bedroom on the second floor can be sitting on top of a larger kitchen or family room below. However, growing horizontally may result in the loss of outdoor space and impact the access to natural light to interior spaces.

And yet additions to a home are not limited to alterations of the building itself; residential properties can also grow by incorporating accessory structures. Commonly seen as garages, these freestanding buildings provide space for uses independent from the rest of the house for entertainment, work, and even for a new dwelling. Habitable accessory structures re-establish the relationships on the use of the outdoors and its distance from the main house while providing extreme privacy from other uses.

The pandemic of 2020 and its concentration of activities into the home has seen a high interest in converting garages and sheds into spaces for learning and working. The intensity of home use highlighted the need for privacy and distance between concurrent activities of different family members. Not just used as new dwellings, accessory structures provide physical distance to add privacy, reduce noise transmission between spaces and lessen artificial light intrusion between spaces.

Efficient compact living in an urban context entails a creative format for residential growth and alterations. A larger structure can accommodate multiple uses and users – from new tenants to full-time employment. While effective and efficient use of residential space, supported by zoning regulations, contributes to reasonable urban growth patterns.

The impact of retail in residential design

The trend to renovate and add spaces to our houses is not new. The design of houses has evolved through time propelled by economic, technical, and technological achievements. The history of the shape of our current homes is still marked by hidden details. Historical changes in bygone eras of retail, work, and travel habits are expressed in the built environment as small gestures.

These days, the discussion of online shopping focuses on the intangible side of retail: the economic impact at local and international levels. But what happens in home design when we shop online? The history of milk delivery is an example of how economic and lifestyle changes have reshaped the size of the home, the location of the kitchen, along with the elements that strengthen the relationship between houses and the rest of the city.

Home milk delivery in the United States became popular with the industrialization of dairy. When American homes had no space for a cow, the milkman became the link to connect the farm with the house. Because residential refrigeration did not become popular until the 1930s, daily frequency of milk delivery remained strong. In fact, refrigerators for residential home use were invented in 1913 but did not become popular until the 1930s. This technological change had a large impact on the design, layout, and use of the kitchen but also it created new relationships with which products, how much, and storage alternatives inside the home.

The combination of private car ownership, residential refrigeration, and bigger grocery stores reduced the dependence on milk delivery. The physical space required to purchase, preserve, and cook dairy reshaped not just the kitchen itself but the connections of the space with the exterior space. The access panels that used to provide a secure and safe space between home and city have been wallpapered since.

When it seemed that the daily transfer of goods between the private and public realm was part of history, online shopping is reshaping how the home interacts with the city for goods and services once again. The internet has re-established the relationship between retail and residential design. Architects did not anticipate the intensity and frequency of online retail and the new space it demands for delivery, storage, and disposal of packing materials. Online retail emphasized the role of home and neighborhood as a participant of the shopping experience; it demands a wider variety of spaces, like porches and alleys that create layers of secure interaction between deliverymen and homeowners.

From doorbells with cameras to secured storage areas, the homes today are the result of the adaptation to the needs and desires of each era. The shape of the neighborhood and the availability of safe transfer of goods and services can be supported through the design of alternative housing features. The evolution of online retail demands a change in the interactions between private and public spaces to satisfy a new relationship between customers and trade.

The social shape of housing

Residential projects are the cultural expression of a social construct. Private design decisions carry a collective weight. The houses we live in are the result of the combination of private and public value. Contemporary design addresses shared challenges, desires, and technical accomplishments.

The 21st century is reshaping the home to accommodate flexible work and study options, innovative retail alternatives, and entertainment. From unconventional housing layouts to data-based infrastructure, the design of homes of the future has the capacity to contribute affordability and sustainable living. New family formats and the high cost of living are strong drivers of interior subdivision of urban housing.

The current demand for new housing models expresses social and economic trends. The disassociation between demand and the availability of shelter emphasizes the human cost of a pervasive deficit of housing units. Overregulation of zoning rules and a history of racist financial practices has contributed to the disconnection between social needs and housing shortage.

An example of this misunderstanding on the human value for shelter and the built environment can be seen in Prince George's County in Maryland, a neighbor to Washington, DC. And is similar to counties surrounding high-cost urban areas throughout the United States today.

Prince George's County is poorer than neighboring counties that surround Washington, DC but it's not uniformly poor. This condition is typical of suburbs and regions in metropolitan areas in the United States. Significant portions have median incomes that are upper middle class, but in areas within the beltway, on the border with Washington, DC, there are pockets of lower income population. Their diversity of wealth is also reflected in differences of urban density. Areas that were served by the historic network of trolleys and regional trains have significantly higher density than those that were not. The county is famous today for being home of a majority African American population with the highest median household income of any county in the United States with over 100,000 residents. However, early in the 20th century it was a majority white county, including some suburbs that were all-white communities.

Black homeowners, particularly in Prince George's County, were particularly hard hit by the 2008 subprime mortgage crisis as Maryland was the third state in the country for foreclosures. The lack of housing options, added to financial predatory practices, emphasized the demand for innovative and safe housing supply. Even if the county today does not have enough housing options to accommodate the needs of their current and future residents, there are zoning limits that ban the creation of new housing by homeowners.

This lack of innovative housing options is the result of an outdated approach to housing solutions. In the same county, the current zoning regulation allows any homeowner to add a garage to their backyard but bans the addition of dwellings in existing properties, even if the resulting structure were to be identical in shape and size to a garage. The right of housing cars instead of people has a concrete impact on the ability of neighbors to provide alternative housing options. This housing-versus-parking reality is almost universal in most counties in the United States.

Low-impact projects, like renovating garages into granny flats, have the ability to provide solutions to the current housing stock deficit while addressing new family formats and social trends of car ownership and usage. Garages can make good homes. A one-bedroom apartment is comparable in size to a two-car garage in footprint and height.

The ability to create affordable housing is related to the relevance that each jurisdiction dedicates to a balanced approach to the use of available private land. Based on many American zoning regulations today, housing cars is more valuable than housing people.

Housing vulnerability

The pandemic of 2020, like many financial and health crises of the past, has exposed the housing vulnerability throughout the world. Even before this health crisis, a large proportion of the United States population lived with such precarious housing safety that the loss of a job could mean homelessness within a month of losing their income. In 2019, 20% of Americans reported no money set aside for dealing with the costs of an unexpected emergency expense. In fact, more than 30% of working adults were three paychecks away from financial disaster. Current housing stock, their layout, and suburban distribution have demonstrated to be poor contributors of shelter in moments of crisis.

Most importantly, negative economic impacts during crises are unevenly distributed throughout the city where homogeneous housing creates pockets of concentrated poverty. The short- and long-term consequences of a crisis becomes harder to overcome when housing options are poorly distributed in urban areas. Affordable housing within established neighborhoods can bolster coordination between social services, quality education, and job options. A school with quality aftercare services can be fundamental in the life of a child experiencing housing insecurity and homelessness. The adaptation of the existing housing stock creates new formats of affordable housing within neighborhoods while integrating them to existing services and infrastructure.

House and family: how to adapt

Just like houses can adapt to new products like cars and refrigerators, houses have the capacity to adapt to new cultural and social trends, like smaller families and new working habits. Oversized residential structures have the potential to introduce flexibility in the use of interior space.

For example, often empty guest rooms can become full-time offices and a basement can be converted into a family room. As the family ages, the corner room on the main floor can be a toy room when the kids are little, a study for adult parents, and eventually can serve as a bedroom for elderly parents that have difficulty navigating stairs. An effective use of space and its flexibility optimizes the overall size of the home in the long term. The sub-occupation of space is expensive and environmentally unsustainable.

Living in efficient homes contributes to reduced living costs. A smaller home is economic in its initial investment but also reduces maintenance and utility costs. Also, when smaller houses are clustered together, they increase density and contribute to a better pedestrian environment that supports local businesses.

The average size of new homes built in the United States grew from 1,660 square feet in 1970 to 2,687 square feet in 2015. That is 62% in 40 years. This growth in residential size goes in the opposite direction of historic family-type trends. During the same period, the average number of people in a household shrank from 3.14 in 1970 to 2.53 in 2015.

To distribute residential space effectively is fundamental to prioritize the use of rooms and the objects that support human activities. Every use of interior space needs to answer the question on how to optimize the overall size of the home.

Innovative housing and levels of privacy

Private space is made up of all spaces within the property lines. They can be indoors, like bedrooms and bathrooms, or outdoors, like a patio or garden. On the other hand, public spaces are those areas shared with others, like the street or a park. Between private and public spaces, a series of layers of transitional spaces control levels of privacy, security, and access among a small group of people. The porch and the front yard of a house are examples of semi-public spaces, they are open to the elements and visually accessible to others, while contributing a level of ownership and security.

Innovative housing design creates new layers in the continuum between public and private spaces. A granny flat in the garden opens the private backyard to be shared with multiple families. Even if limited to just the occupants of the property, this new outdoor space welcomes shared activities. Multiple dwellings located in a single lot can control levels of privacy by introducing landscape and hardscape design features.

In a shared private outdoor space, small children can seek care without venturing outside, if the nanny lives in the property. Older adults who live in a house in the backyard can enjoy the outdoors without the physical burden of maintenance associated to traditional single-family homes.

When different sized homes share public and semi-private spaces, the dynamic of those members also changes. People unable to live independently can have privacy, indoors and outdoors, while receiving care from in-unit neighbors. People of different economic backgrounds can share the safety of a large backyard by exchanging services.

The example of how small children "age" into the use of the interior space can also be seen in how that age affects the use of outdoor spaces around the house and throughout the city. Safety, independence, and self-sufficiency are feasible when we incorporate new types of housing into the existing fabric of the city.

New porches, smaller and denser front yards, shared sidewalks are the public expression of innovative housing typologies. The current deficit of the housing stock can be satisfied when we bypass discussions about parking, and we observe how cultural and economic forces shape the houses needed today.

Semi-spaces: from private to public

The vibrancy of residential space is not just determined by space enclosed by four walls and a roof but is also enhanced by its relationship to the city. How each home connects to others, to the sidewalk, and to public services like parks and schools, strengthens public participation and social bonds. The vitality of urban life is also nurtured by the relationship between different housing typologies in the same area.

For the relationship between public and private spaces to become an enriching experience, the transition from indoors to outdoors must be organized by a sequence of interstitial spaces. These semi-spaces reinforce behavior and enrich the civic experience of the public domain. From absolutely private, like a bedroom, to absolutely public, like a city park, humans inhabit a series of demi-spaces that condition individual and social behavior. Those demi-spaces are the result of visual and physical clues that determine ownership.

The private space is the exclusive space of the residents of a property. It can be outdoors or indoors. The physical features of the building envelope provide safety and visual privacy from the public realm. The public space is the urban environment accessible to the general public with no limitation on the duration of occupancy. Even when there is a level of government control of the public space, such as streets or parks, public space is physically and visually accessible to all. Each stage of the sequence between the public sphere and the private property is determined by the capacity of each individual to control and define an area that will contribute to their quality of life.

A semi-private space is the area of controlled access by residents and guests. For example, the hallway in a condominium is a semi-private space, only those with access to the building – residents and guests – can occupy it. Even if the space is not fully private, a limited group of people can reach it physically and visually. Semi-private spaces allow for a level of safety and privacy different from fully private spaces, like an apartment unit. Occupants of each apartment can leave a pair of shoes or a wet umbrella in the hallway by the door and expect to find them there in the morning. Semi-private spaces can be outdoors as well, a driveway you share with neighbors can be the place you leave your bicycle unlocked and garden tools overnight.

Along with semi-private spaces, the transition from private to public is made up by the semi-public space. Semi-public spaces provide security and visual privacy but are open to individuals who do not belong in the household. These spaces allow for design interventions to be shared with others. From a bench to a flag, the semi-public space adds a layer of ownership, and creates a safe space between the home and the city.

The semi-public space is the area physically accessible to the general public but controlled by the property owners. A store or a restaurant is an example of semi-public space that houses businesses. In residential design, the front porch of a house is an example of a semi-public space. Under the porch roof, the homeowners allow access to the public, such as the mailman, but also control the time that the occupancy can take place. Semi-public spaces are visually open to the public way but privately owned and controlled. They provide security and are visually filtered from the public view. Design interventions are seen in semi-public spaces by adding comfort features, like swings, that enhance the socialization between the private and public spaces.

Even when lot lines are the legal separation between properties, there are opportunities to create filters and spaces that enhance this transition. From the sidewalk to the door, there are a series of spaces shaped like stoops, gardens, and porches that hold demi-spaces. Far from a solid wall that determines ownership, residential design can contribute gestures that enhance this transition and improve the public realm.

The wealth of the transition between private and public space is weaker in environments with homogeneous low-density housing, like the suburbs. The lack of sidewalks, front porches, and other physical expressions of demi-spaces create an invisible barrier between the public and the home. Urban environments with filters between private and public spaces contribute to social interaction. Sidewalk cafes, store windows, and porches strengthen the relationship between humans that inhabit those spaces. Heterogeneous housing size and shapes provide design opportunities of demi-spaces. A converted garage's door becomes a porch for an elderly resident. A granny flat adds visual security to an alley. Alternative housing formats within the existing urban network improves the perception of the public space.

Design features like landscape, gates, stairs, and other architectural elements contribute to a sense of ownership with collaboration between residents and neighbors. Good urban design and creative zoning rules create opportunities to share private and public spaces between citizens. The addition of innovative housing design has the potential to create new physical spaces that enrich urban interactions.

CHAPTER 6

Innovation and Additional Dwelling Units

What is an additional dwelling unit?

An additional dwelling unit (ADU) is a smaller, independent residential dwelling located on the same lot as an existing single-family home. They are known under different names, such as accessory apartments, secondary suites, and granny flats. These units can be converted from a portion of a home, like the basement, or in a detached structure, like the garage. These units add a new variety of housing types in established neighborhoods.

The addition of dwellings within the existing housing stock has a series of benefits. They have a positive contribution to the local economy by creating direct and indirect jobs during construction. After the building has been completed, the land improvement and the addition of residential square footage increases monetary value of the overall property. Moreover, secondary units represent a positive fiscal impact on the tax base of housing in the city.

The main influence of additional dwelling units at a community level is the creation of alternative housing options different from the typical single-family homes. Secondary units also contribute to low-impact density benefit from established infrastructure and services, such as transit and schools.

Particularly for multigenerational households, additional dwelling units benefit homeowners by utilizing surplus private space as contributor of companionship and care, along with reduced cost of housing for the elderly. Most importantly, the additional income contributes to housing stability in times of crisis, especially for those living on a fixed income.

The nature of secondary units, different from a typical rental apartment, offers the opportunity for an exchange of formal and informal services, from paid duties like childcare to supplemental help in maintenance, such as shoveling snow and yard work.

Tenants of additional dwelling units benefit from access to well-established neighborhood housing and service options. By introducing smaller, more affordable units within existing neighborhoods, the housing market offers new opportunities for less affluent families to access good schools and public services typically available in wealthier areas of the city.

Additional dwelling units as an innovative housing typology offers layered benefits to homeowners, tenants, and municipalities that contribute positive social and economic synergy.

Lifecycle of shelter

As people age and their families evolve in size, additional dwelling units play a significant role in the occupation of the property. This extra unit within the home adds variety in the use of space. Different from moving from house to house and uprooting neighborhood, the smaller unit balances the approach of home based on space needs.

For example, a first-time homebuyer may have access to a fixer upper property. The layout of a single-family home with a freestanding garage offers the opportunity to phase the improvements of the property as funds become available.

In this example, the homebuyer can repair the garage first in order to make it habitable while the rest of the house is fixed. When the main house is complete, she can move in as her family grows. The converted garage that housed her at the beginning of the homeownership process welcomes another adult for childcare support.

As these children age and childcare may be less demanding, the original garage can provide rental income from a tenant, adding financial support to the overall cost of living. As the family ages and the younger generation leave the house for college, the original secondary unit can provide housing for aging parents. Later in life, this unit can also contribute a housing option to boomerang children, burdened with students' loans but ready to live independently.

As the original homeowner ages and her own physical abilities are diminished, she may want to occupy the garage once again and benefit from the lack of stairs and compact living options. The main house can be rented to others as a larger financial contributor to household expenses.

In this case, the layout of two houses in the same property accommodates an ever-evolving family dynamic of size, age, and physical ability of its members. As families age, the demand for quantity and quality of space also develops through each individual's life.

Housing shape, family dynamics and finances demonstrate that the evolution of housing options and affordability are the result of a proactive understanding of shelter. Age and time can become a positive contributor to home occupancy if the innovative housing type supports an evolving lifestyle.

How innovative housing contributes value

The subdivision of a private property contributes a stable financial incentive in the long term. Most of the potential clients that call my office to discuss the addition of units to their house are interested in the financial impact and contribution to their property. As part of a larger social trend of bringing relatives to live closer to the family, homeowners want to make sure that the money invested will pay off in the long term.

Because of the existing housing stock in Washington, DC, where I work, most of the additional dwelling units occur in basements and small garages in the rear. The process to plan, design and build a new unit balances the scope of work, the timeline for the family, and the budget. In those initial calls we discuss what the project will consist of, how long it will take to complete, and how much it will cost once it is finished.

Garage conversions in Washington, DC illustrate the typical process of transforming a sub-occupied space, for parking and storage, into housing. A few years ago, when a client called my office to discuss converting her garage into an additional dwelling unit, the structure seemed pretty typical for this region. The garage, originally built by a previous homeowner, had been built to park a boat. Yes, parking a boat in Washington, DC!

The building resulted in an additional dwelling unit distributed in two levels along with covered one-car parking on the ground floor. The contributing value of the original boat-garage to the family finances had been monetarily marginal. In fact, the commercial value of indoor parking in that particular residential area was negligible to the value of the home. In general, where street parking is plentiful, like in this boat-garage project, the conversion of a structure from parking to housing adds to the net value of a house.

This renovation and the growth of rentable habitable space illustrates how the residential capacity to house a car (or a boat) in an urban environment is not a financial contributor to real estate value compared to the capacity to house people.

The challenges of additional dwelling units

The current crisis in affordable housing and the ongoing deficit of dwelling units in cities and suburbs highlights the need to re-evaluate the use of private spaces. Additional dwelling units in existing basements and garages contribute to the city's density and intensity of use by welcoming new neighbors.

Additional dwelling units, as a housing typology, can be organized within the existing legal framework of renting and buying property. Leasing is the typical format for private individuals to share their property because it grants use of portions of the house while limiting access to others. Each party in the relationship has rights of usage, with conditions relating to certain responsibilities like upkeep and security. However, current overly restrictive zoning regulations and homeowners' associations condition who can occupy a residential private property and how.

Historically, rental properties have been considered less valuable than those properties occupied by owners. Housing was divided into two large groups: owner-occupied suburban family homes and rental urban apartments. The challenge of introducing additional dwelling units into single-family homes requires a shift in the paradigm of the significance of ownership. This new typology brings together homeowners and renters within the property. What happens if the property is both owner- and renter-occupied? Innovative housing typologies for modern family types require a cultural shift on how properties received monetary value separate from the occupant that lives in it.

The occupancy of additional dwelling units is already defined in the rights and obligations of landlord and tenant laws of cities across the nation. The implementation of alternative housing does not require the reinvention of home, nor the way we share them with others.

The resistance of homeowners' associations to the implementation of additional dwelling units has argued that alternative housing increases traffic, lowers property values, and contributes to school overcrowding. With the argument to "defend single-family homes" homeowners' associations restrict the transformation of garages and basements into affordable units within established neighborhoods. Regions where accessory dwelling units are allowed by right have not exacerbated any of those concerns.

During the 2019 council debates in Montgomery County in Maryland in anticipation of approving additional dwelling unit zoning changes, protesters who opposed the change marched into the council headquarters with signs. A letter to the editor published in the Washington Post even argued that it would convert the county into a slum. Opponents of additional dwelling units in established neighborhoods, mostly organized around homeowners' and civic associations, typically see this change in zoning as an attack on the American Dream. Montgomery County amended its zoning laws to make it easier to build accessory apartments in a 9 to 0 vote.

How to subdivide a property

Subdividing a property is a long-term venture. The cost of construction alone requires planning that balances the worth of the house, its equity, and the potential for income. From an individual's perspective, the implementation of an additional dwelling unit is a real estate investment. Additional dwelling units create a new house, minus the cost of the land.

Additional dwelling units can be located within the existing house or detached from it. This will affect levels of privacy, access to the natural light, and limit the potential for future alterations.

An additional dwelling unit as a basement apartment takes advantage of an existing sub-occupied space, access to the street, and existing building envelope. By reusing foundation walls, structural elements and party walls, the basement optimizes the building's interior space and has limited impact on the building's presence on the street. Despite its architectural challenges, basement units are ideal formats of additional dwelling units in townhouses with limited yards in high-cost urban areas.

However, one of the main drawbacks of implementing a basement apartment is the loss of privacy. Sharing floor and ceiling with the main house can easily transmit noise between units. Depending on site conditions, a basement can pose a challenge to access for people with disabilities. Because of their tight urban conditions, the resulting below-ground interior space is not always a contributor of quality natural light.

The implementation of basement apartments also limits the potential growth of the house. Depending on the size of the above-ground floor plan, by excluding the basement for living space, the house may become too small for a growing family in the future.

Aside from basements, additional dwelling units can capture a portion of the main house. Oversized floor plates can be subdivided into smaller units to accommodate new dwellings at street level. Dedicating a portion of a house to an apartment provides access to the front and rear of the property, contributes natural light, and adds privacy for its occupants.

Aside from basements and subdivision of existing homes, additional dwelling units can also be the result of the occupation of an accessory structure. Accessory structures are considered any building external to the main house, like a refurbished garage or a workshop. The main advantage of creating a dwelling in a detached structure is this distance to the main house as a contributor of privacy and independent use. These types of structure, historically accessible for cars, creates opportunities for barrier-free housing from the public way to the home accessible for people with disabilities. Adding a dwelling unit physically separate from the main house has the advantage of preserving all existing features of the original structure. It also allows for future alterations of the main house as homeowners may need it.

One of the main drawbacks of refurbished accessory structures, however, is that the distance from the main house and the public way increases the cost of infrastructure, such as water and sewage connections. Despite the popularity of this freestanding housing format, additional dwelling units in the backyard also condition the use of the outdoors by members of each household. Depending on the size of the property and the volume of each building, new accessory structures may interfere with access to views and natural light.

The planning of an additional dwelling unit within an existing property demands a feasibility study on the short- and long-term impact on the use of the house. Each option will have cost and lifestyle implications based on the location, the conditions of the existing building, and the infrastructure required to operate both homes.

Where to start: understanding users

The shape of the additional dwelling unit will reflect its users. Who is this building for? How long will she/he be there? How many people will live in it? How about 10 years after construction is complete? Early questions in the design process outline project choices. To understand users of residential projects, it is important to focus on how the age, lifestyle, and size of the family will shape the building.

The occupants' age is one of the stronger factors to determine occupancy of an additional dwelling unit. For example, if the people who will occupy the building are a couple over 60 years old, exterior stairs to reach an apartment above the garage may not be the ideal layout. To support aging in place, an accessory unit must offer easy interior navigation and barrier-free connections to the outside. In the example of exterior stairs, this feature alone will expose users to the elements and add challenges between levels. However, if the unit is designed to be occupied by a college student, accessibility is less critical.

The aspect of family size also shapes additional dwelling units. If the intent is to accommodate a family with small children, the location and distribution of individual and common spaces will organize the interior. Access to the outdoors as an area of play will also establish the relationship with the main house.

To focus on the main and earliest uses of an additional dwelling unit is the result of conscientious design discussions. Who will use the kitchen? How will the residents navigate stairs? Early design decisions are crucial for the long-term operation of the unit.

Plan, design, and build: long-term implications

The first step to consider in the implementation of an additional dwelling unit is to understand the conditions of a site, the relationship to the existing home, and financial implications of the investment. Different from purchasing a car, once a building is complete, it becomes expensive to make significant changes in the short term. In residential construction, short term is a decade. Early decisions in the design process of an additional dwelling unit will also affect the timeline of repairs and alterations.

An additional dwelling unit, despite its small size, should be designed and built to last. Using good quality materials and tested construction methods will provide durability of the building and better interior spaces. Thoughtful design will result in efficient spaces and allow for flexibility in the future.

For example, structural elements like the building envelope should not require maintenance in 50 years, if ever. Windows and doors may be worth upgrading after 20 years to benefit from environmental contributions of new technologies. Mechanical systems such as boilers and air conditioning every 20, and finishes, like tiles and flooring, should last a minimum of a decade. The lifespan of each building system shows that early decisions will save money in the long term. From building layout to infrastructure, the additional dwelling unit can reduce energy consumption and maintenance cost. With proper care and maintenance, the lifespan of a house is about 200 years; in comparison, the average lifespan of a car is 12.

How to subdivide a house

Most houses can accommodate an additional dwelling unit by adding space. However, the existing housing stock can also accommodate a new unit by repurposing under-occupied interior space.

A house can be subdivided horizontally where each level becomes a new unit. For by-level redesign to be feasible, vertical circulation and hallway distribution will be fundamental to organize private and common uses of interior space. Challenges of multilevel subdivisions include emergency egress, access to the public way, and efficient distribution of infrastructure.

For example, a simple subdivision of a townhouse into two units can be organized around a small vestibule. However, a four-level home will have to reorganize stairs and hallways to effectively manage access to each unit. The number of units at each level will also condition the size and location of infrastructure necessary to operate the building. Access to the public way of horizontally divided homes can be distributed around the main floor or concentrated in the main entrance.

Houses can also be subdivided vertically where each unit contains its own stairs and independent access to the public way or backyard. A home with a large floor plate could accommodate four units where each occupies a corner of the house. This subdivision will provide multiple options to connect to the outdoors at ground level, like a wrap-around porch, and less shared spaces for circulation.

The main challenge of subdividing a structure vertically is the repetition of circulation spaces for adjacent units. The fact that each apartment will have multiple levels also means that each homeowner will have to dedicate a significant portion to internal vertical circulation. However, houses that are subdivided vertically can provide multiple points of entry from the street, creating independent access points from the public way.

Aside from vertical and horizontal partitioning, houses can also be subdivided within the lot they sit in. Multiple smaller buildings within a lot can share outdoor spaces, such as patios, parking, and infrastructure like car charging stations, barbecue grilles or pools. The creation of multiple separate units within a lot are known as "villages" or "commons." The main advantage of this layout is the opportunity to introduce variety in the size and design of units. These types of grouped housing often develop around a common interest and beneficial relationship between neighbors. They are popular among friends, families with children, and multigenerational households. These types of multiple housing units within a property often known as "co-living," are describing a type of intentional community that provides shared housing. From cost savings to shared interests, these building types welcome a variety of ages and family types.

The creative subdivision of the existing housing stock contributes new shapes to the current deficit of units. The resulting gentle density preserves the existing character of established neighborhoods and reduces the impact of large housing projects.

What is old is new again: Takoma Park

The effort to subdivide existing housing stock is not new. It has been exercised in the past to address housing needs to changing social and economic trends. Takoma Park in Maryland was the first suburb in the Washington DC area. Founded within walking distance of a train station, it was planned as an oasis compared to the swampy malaria ridden capital city.

When walking around Takoma Park today, it is evident that the original housing stock experienced significant changes throughout history. Initially planned as single-family homes surrounded by generous greenery, after World War II the units were subdivided into multiple apartments and utilized as rooming housing. Buoyed by the intense activity at Walter Reed Hospital, nurses increased demand for housing options which resulted in the subdivision of houses into smaller apartments.

Later in the century, a local ban on multihousing options by Montgomery County, where Takoma Park sits, resulted in the reversal of multi-units into single-family homes. Even for those homeowners that wanted to develop units within their properties, they were subject to an extensive process and application for special exceptions to the zoning code. This obscure process banned the practice of creating additional dwelling units in the county for almost 40 years.

In 2019, the housing deficit and increased cost of living in the region brought in new legislation where additional dwelling units became legal and feasible once again. The new regulation removed restrictions such as density of units per block, and eliminated minimum lot size requirements. It also reduced the number of parking spaces required even if it retained some level of on-site parking requirements.

The new legislation on additional dwelling units today promotes the approval and inspection of unlicensed existing units, remnants of prior apartments from the housing stock of the 1950s. The licensing of existing units allows informal housing units to become part of the city inspection program that provides healthy and safe conditions for renters.

The historic evolution of housing types in Takoma Park and Montgomery County illustrates how the abstract concepts of zoning regulations shape the economy and access to housing in the region.

Neighborhood resistance

The implementation of additional dwelling units as a normal type of housing option is a paradigm shift from the typical American single-family home format. Despite the benefits of accessory apartments as generators of affordable housing for families, there is still a resistance to implement this housing typology in established neighborhoods.

Because zoning regulations are the result of a social construct, community meetings where housing topics are covered are fueled by neighbors concerned with home values, school overcrowding, traffic, and neighborhood character. Pedestrian and vehicular traffic, along with the capacity to share public infrastructure, are at the forefront of debates about where and how to create alternative and affordable housing.

Community meetings around zoning regulations are sources of high-conflict conversation where cultural, economic, and racial misconceptions are expressed openly behind ideas of affordability, economic status, and the physical expression of single-family homes.

For example, during the council meetings in Montgomery County, some of the topics covered by local residents emphasized the hypothetical negative impact of the number of doors each house would be allowed to face the street with. Even if there is no health or safety reason that justifies the ban of multiple pedestrian entry points into a private residence, the argument weighted on the contributing value of an additional door facing the street. From porches to windows and greenery, residential structures already contribute a wide variety of elements that enrich the character of the street. The limitation of entry doors into a property as a design item to be regulated by zoning is misguided and inconsequential to the capacity of a neighborhood to welcome a wider variety of families.

Aside from the physical expression of additional dwelling units, parking is the most contentious topic during zoning discussions about affordable housing. As single-family homes convert into multiple units, the potential to attract more cars to the neighborhood stresses the need of public transit and alternative modes of travel, from proper sidewalks to safe bike lanes. In fact, occupants of smaller units located close to transit and healthy walking environments are less likely to own multiple cars per family unit.

Another common fear during public discussion about zoning and housing is the potential of school overcrowding. However, multiple studies show no correlation between housing production and school enrollment growth. Even if children occupy new housing units, they produce a marginal change in enrollment at local schools. When considering additional dwelling units in an established neighborhood, the rate of housing growth is not a useful predictor of school enrollment change. However, other demographic trends, such as parental preferences and school quality, are stronger influencers of educational demand.

Neighborhood concerns about subdividing single-family homes to provide additional dwelling units are also focused on the over demand for existing utility services. This myth is dispelled when we compare an aging home versus the creation of a new unit. Efficient appliances reduce consumption of water and energy, better insulation demands less electricity to condition interior spaces, higher density housing reduces the demand of car usage. Smaller and better distributed housing options are less demanding to urban infrastructure and the environment than oversized suburban options.

Increasing density in established neighborhoods contributes to an efficient use of existing public infrastructure and services. Existing transit and metro can gain riders. From schools to parks, from public lighting to bus shelters, gentle density optimizes the use of public space and the tax funds necessary to maintain it. Innovative housing typologies contribute "eyes on the street," riders of public transit, and active participants to the local economy.

Urban living and homelessness

What would happen if nothing changed? What are the consequences of maintaining the status quo in housing design and production? How bad can it get? How fast?

Urban housing is one of the largest contributors of living expenses. The U.S. Department of Housing and Urban Development (HUD) uses a threshold of 30% of the gross income to determine whether a house is affordable. Individuals who spend more than 30% of their income on housing are considered cost-burdened.

Options for housing accessibly is strongly connected to the availability of housing types, their location, and the quality of life that will result from the surrounding environment. Today, not only are there few housing choices for the poor, but those units are served by worse performing schools and are located in environments with higher crime and more sources of pollution. Homogeneous housing distribution organized by existing zoning regulations exacerbates the lack of access to quality services for the poor.

In 2019, the median income in large cities in the United States was not enough for the average person to avoid being cost-burdened. In San Francisco, California, the average monthly rent for a two-bedroom apartment is $4,600, about $55,000 a year. A household in San Francisco needs to earn about $197,000 to avoid being cost-burdened. The median household income in San Francisco was $112,376. Also, pockets of high-income earners, like Silicon Valley, exacerbate the income inequality in California making it the highest in the nation.

Homelessness is not just lack of housing but also housing that is below the minimum standard of living to provide safe shelter. Homeless people are those living on the streets, moving between temporary shelters, including those of family and friends, and those individuals living in housing conditions that lack sanitary infrastructure and cooking facilities. People who experience homelessness suffer from worse physical and mental health outcomes. Even if the root causes of homelessness are nuanced and require a multidiscipline approach, a significant factor in the increase of homelessness is the lack of housing options located near services and jobs.

Between 2007 and 2010, family homelessness in the United States increased by 20%. Over a million schoolchildren were homeless in the 2011-2012 school year, a 75%

increase since 2007. At the same time, a rise in homeless encampments emerged in cities across the United States. These encampments are the public expression of rising living costs and the demand of social services for individuals experiencing financial and mental health crises. Proximity and convenience to healthcare options, jobs, and potential for income are the undercurrent behind tent cities located in the urban environment.

In California alone, despite its wealth, more than 150,000 residents were homeless in 2019. Even when mental health, addiction, trauma, and interaction with the criminal justice system are factors that affect an individual's capacity to access housing, the primary reason for homelessness remains cost: individuals' inability to afford rent. Fueled by decades of underproduction in California, the number of older affordable housing units is declining, and government subsidized housing has not filled the gap to satisfy the current demand.

When additional dwelling units are created, along with other denser housing options, existing urban areas increases affordability in two ways. On one hand it creates a new unit that did not exist before. On the other hand, where the additional dwelling unit sits becomes more affordable for the homeowners by reducing their cost of living.

I use the term "to grow within" to refer to the alterations that allow families to thrive in their home throughout life stages. To grow within is to optimize the use of a home that results in supportive spaces, improve its relationship to the outdoors, and allow individuals to participate in civic life. The creation of additional dwelling units within the existing housing stock increases the capacity of each family to grow within their property by reducing cost of living and opening possibilities to create affordable housing for others.

Additional dwelling units as an investment

From a homeowner's perspective, additional dwelling units are a real estate investment. These projects follow market trends when it comes to valuation, initial costs, and amortization. The initial expense of a project is significant for the homeowners; even with regional variations, the starting cost of a one-bedroom unit can easily exceed $100,000.

The main benefit of the additional dwelling unit as a real estate investment is the shared cost of land and services with a property already owned. Even when calculated the increased tax base for the improved property, the yearly income generated by the new dwelling can exceed the increased fiscal cost.

Fannie Mae, the underwriter of home mortgages in the United States, currently recognizes the monetary contribution of additional dwelling units to the existing value of the house. The organization outlines building and infrastructure requirements of an accessory structure to be assessed as a dwelling and differentiate from other home renovation projects. Fannie Mae also influences design choices and zoning regulations by requiring the additional dwelling unit to be smaller than the main house, and limits the addition of dwellings to one. With this limit, the financial organization excludes multiple additional dwelling units from being created from the subdivision of a home, such as a basement and a garage simultaneously.

Even if local zoning regulations were to change to allow more affordable housing developed by homeowners, current financial models exclude this possibility to create units. Unless more financial options become available, the housing stock is still limited to just one additional unit per property even if they are architecturally ready to provide more.

Due to the new format of this housing typology, there is still no formal method to assign worth to a property with an additional dwelling unit. Appraisers struggle to assign monetary value to this new housing due to lack of historical comparative units in a region. The sales comparison approach requires multiple recent sales of similar properties.

An alternative to the existing financial method, in order to value additional dwelling units and promote their development, would be an income-based valuation. This type of valuation derives worth for income-producing property by converting its anticipated benefits into the property value. For example, when assessing the value of a loan to finance the construction of a one-bedroom unit, appraisers can look at the rental value of apartments in the area. The format of housing – apartment vs granny flat – can generate comparable income even if the building is shaped differently. However, due to the unpredictability of rental markets, appraisers find it challenging to provide an anticipated monetary value for an additional dwelling unit owned by individuals different from owners of large apartment buildings.

Housing and zoning dynamics, along with contradictory language between loan originators and appraisers, remains a barrier to the valuation of additional dwelling units. Their assessment remains overly conservative in most markets, cementing the difficulties to implement these projects in the real world.

Options to finance

Because the construction of additional dwelling units is so onerous, there is a series of financial options to approach the project. Most of my clients, when facing significant renovation projects, finance the project using cash and some other financial product. Depending on each individual situation, a careful analysis of potential income, property worth, and budget for construction can result in significant differences of return on investment in the long term.

The first financial option and the most common approach today is a home equity line of credit (HELOC). How does it work? If the homeowner owns enough of the property and it is deemed valuable enough, the bank allows the homeowner to borrow against it. Loans are subject to interest and the property is the collateral. Because there is no separate title for an additional dwelling unit, both units will be part of the same collateral.

The second option to finance the construction of additional dwelling units is a cash out refinance of an existing mortgage. This model allows homeowners to borrow in smaller amounts when funds are needed. Depending on the valuation of the property and current interest rates, this option can be feasible when accounting for the income generated by the new additional dwelling unit. Money is borrowed and spent on the property as multiple projects occur on the site, from a new dwelling to an interior renovation of the main house.

The third option, informally called construction loans, is an avenue for funds that requires coordination between architect, contractor, and lender. It provides the funds representative of the completed value of the additional dwelling unit. Even if it requires no money down, the financing is released as the work on site is completed. Because of the increased timeline for payments, the cost of construction may increase compared to other financing options.

The fourth option, FHA (203k) and Fannie Mae through HomeStyle loans are available for primary residences. Those loans are ideal for first-time home buyers in need of funds to immediately renovate their properties. Interest rates and limitations on the type and timeline of work vary greatly per project.

An example of an innovative financial model is found in the Los Angeles non-profit organization LA Más, called "Backyard Homes Project." It supports the creation of more affordable housing units for housing voucher recipients. This program offers optional financing, design, permitting, construction, and leasing support to build and rent a new unit. With community education programs and professional assistance, LA Más has developed design samples and financial tools that contribute to the feasibility of additional dwelling units for homeowners.

As part of a wider effort to improve community building projects, LA Más developed a project in the Highland Park neighborhood that resulted in a home with an additional dwelling unit included in the original design. The project was so successful that it received an award from the Los Angeles Business Council. The triumph of the project was the result of the collaboration between non-profit organizations like Habitat for Humanity, professional designers, and community involvement.

The demand for additional dwelling units has increased innovative forms of financing that are in early stages of development, from land lease to sweat-equity contributions. Still, financial challenges for low-income earners and distressed properties remain barriers to create more housing units that can revitalize neighborhoods in underinvested areas.

About rentals

Innovative housing options are not just the result of volunteer or good intentioned citizens. Concrete financial rules of the built environment, from initial cost to return on investments, apply to additional dwelling units. These spaces are long-term and low-risk investments. In these units the homeowner has more flexibility to adapt the cost of leasing to a fluctuating local market. Areas with high tourist interest may benefit from short-term rentals. Those looking to occupy the building for parts of the year can benefit from seasonal occupants, like winter snowbirds in Florida. Homeowners looking for a traditional renter-landlord relationship can welcome tenants with long-term leases.

The financial contribution of additional dwelling units is similar to other rental properties: all applicable laws to tenancy of a traditional property apply. From lease to eviction, from noise to safety, the relationship between homeowner and tenants is organized through established laws that protect both parties.

However, many jurisdictions place limits on the implementation of additional dwelling units for short-term tenancy. The popularity of house renting applications has had an impact on the availability of housing options. Even when there are economic benefits for local economies from tourism, the costs of short-term house sharing outweigh its benefits in local housing markets. Similar to gentrification, the "Airbnb effect" is where the slow increase value of an area is detrimental to the indigenous residents.

Popular cities like Amsterdam, Barcelona, and Los Angeles are victims of this type of over tourism that has a negative impact on house pricing and community. This effect is also having a detrimental impact on housing stock as it encourages landlords to move their properties from long-term to short-term tenancy. To reduce the impact of the Airbnb effect, municipalities are exploring options like fees for short-term rentals, licenses and owner occupancy requirements for additional dwelling units.

Reality check: building and zoning regulations

Additional dwelling units are subject to all building and zoning regulations just like a single-family home is. Each jurisdiction may provide a different technical name for them but, in general, they are labeled as "accessory structures" or "accessory apartments" to differentiate them from condominiums or apartment buildings.

The compliance with all building and zoning rules may add cost to the implementation of additional dwelling units. And yet, there is a long-term value to use tested materials and systems that can perform in the long term.

I have seen in Washington, DC how the proliferation of "ghost" apartments has dotted the city. Those apartments are unregistered units that comply with parts of the building code but dangerously exclude others, such as properly sized window egress. When visiting projects that anticipate a renovation, I am mostly concerned on how to add value through aesthetics and efficiency but also safety. Most of these unregulated ghost units are made up of basement apartments from another era, that due to economic pressure and increased housing demand have been transformed into illegal dwellings.

Current housing stock is ruled by two major overlapping

rule books: the zoning rules and the building code. To easily differentiate the application of each rule book, we must only look at the building envelope as the divider between the interior and exterior space and it is made up of the roof, walls, and floor.

The building code is concerned with all elements that affect the building envelope and the interior. The zoning regulations are concerned with the building envelope in relation to its neighbors.

Zoning rules are extremely local. They set limits on setbacks, from streets and neighbors, amount of green space, and height of buildings. Each neighborhood and street has its own values set by local jurisdictions. Zoning regulations for most municipalities can be found online today.

Building rules, on the other hand, are almost universally applied in the United States. In fact, the first building code was created in 1905 by an insurance group, the National Board of Fire Underwriters, to minimize risk to property and building occupants. A variety of regional code organizations was consolidated into the International Code Council that published the first set of codes in 2000. The building code is updated every three years following technical advances and expert advice from the building industry.

The building code is organized by discipline, from general building topics to electrical and mechanical. The building codes are also influenced by cultural and economic forces. For example, in 2010, the International Code Council launched the International Green Construction code to help the construction industry in the implementation of sustainable buildings.

In general, when planning an additional dwelling unit, it is useful to think about zoning regulations as "what if" in a neighborhood. What if I convert my garage into a house? What if I add a two-story building in the rear? Once the zoning analysis shows that it is possible, the building code will organize the "how to" of the new project. How do I attach a railing to this stair? How much insulation I should install? How much can I slope this roof? The complete design process of an additional dwelling unit should flow from a zoning analysis to the specification of window sizes.

Building by systems

I have seen the flashy videos of houses popping up in two hours. Or the crane dropping someone's house in a lot with the ease of putting on a dress. And yet, the current housing deficit is not just a lack of materials or workmanship but a holistic approach of how a systemic approach to land and buildings contributes to affordable housing. It is important to understand that a building will only work if all its systems work in unison. But what are building systems? Why do they matter? Next time you relax in front of the TV to enjoy a house renovation show, you will remember this section.

Buildings work because they are made up of systems that provide shelter and comfort. Systems are organized by their function: site, structure, envelope, infrastructure, equipment, and finishes. Excluding one system or a part of it from the planning of a dwelling has economic and safety consequences for the occupant.

When planning a house or an additional dwelling unit, the site is the main organizer on how a house will be shaped and located. From water drainage to utilities, the land where the building sits will determine a large proportion of the final cost of the project. The building's systems associated with site are all connections to public utilities, from cable boxes to wastewater. Depending on the urban conditions of a site, the cost of all site systems can become onerous.

Another fundamental system is the building envelope. This part of the project is made up of all the elements that separate the interior from the exterior space: walls, roof, and floor. Along with the interior layers that make up each element: windows, doors, and insulation, among many other parts. The building envelope regulates environmental conditions, controls access to natural light, and provides safety. The building envelope is a contributor to the exterior character of a building and is the main regulator of comfort and economy for its occupants.

Different but integrated to the site and the envelope, the structural system is the support of all loads that affect a building. From gravity to wind and earthquakes, structural elements also carry the weight of people and furniture. From roof joists to foundations, this building system requires a strong understanding of local site conditions. Two identical buildings, one located in California and another in Georgia, are likely to have different structural systems to address local seismic and wind conditions.

In order for the building to operate, the infrastructure systems within a home allow the building to work. Environmental controls like heating and cooling, plumbing, and electrical networks are required to sustain comfortable human life. Hidden behind walls: pipes, ducts and cables are expressed through lights, switches, and showerheads around the house.

The last building system that makes up a dwelling is made up by all the finishes. From interior drywall to exterior cladding, from tile to paint, the visible layer of the built environment enhances the perception of interior space, contributes to safety, and protects the interior layers of the building envelope. This system is the aesthetic expression of the owner but also each layer has a function to protect the layer below. The tile in the kitchen backsplash protects the drywall from moisture. The cladding of a house gives it an identity in the neighborhood but also protects the insulation inside the wall. Each surface and material of the building has a role to play.

The relationship between all systems is fundamental to understand cost of construction, building durability, and interior comfort. The comparison between different building methods requires a thoughtful analysis on the integration of each part of the building and how it will affect the occupant in the long term.

Roles in design and construction

In my experience as an architect, I have seen confusion about how to and who to talk when thinking about an additional dwelling unit project. "But... I've never worked with an architect before!" is one of the most common phrases I hear during initial phone calls with potential clients. Small residential projects can be resolved with a design team made up from architect, engineers, and builder. The client will also benefit from conversations with a lender early in the process that assist in the determination of the budget.

The architect drives the design effort, from a feasibility study to outline a budget, scope, and general timeline. The architect works with the "how" of a building: How will the building be shaped? How will the rooms be distributed? How can the environment contribute to interior comfort? How to reach the best views? How much will it cost? A continuous dialogue between client and architect enriches ideas about each question during the design process.

The design and implementation of an additional dwelling unit is neither an imposition nor a sale. The building is the result of a proactive exchange of ideas between space needs and design options. Architects are experts on space and buildings, clients are experts on their own life and needs. The relevance of an architect becomes crucial to navigate local regulations, design ideas, and building code requirements. The more compact the project, the more relevant the role of the architect becomes to enhance the use of space with economy and creativity.

Working alongside the architect, engineers contribute the layout of the structure and the infrastructure of the building. Aside from calculations and sizing, their role brings economy and efficiency to systems. Structural engineers size load-bearing elements, from foundations to roof joists. Electrical engineers lay out circuits that support the operation of the house, from the panel to an electrical car charger. Collaboration between architects and engineers results in an efficient use of resources and enhanced comfort.

Once the architect designs the building, the engineers coordinate their scope of work. This collaboration will result in a set of drawings to be reviewed and approved by the local jurisdiction. The same drawing set can be distributed among different contractors to obtain comparable bids for the construction of the project. General contractors are welcome to the design team as contributors of local expertise in construction methods, material availability, and improved production processes.

Depending on each jurisdiction, the review and approval of drawings can be an expedited or lengthy process. From rural to urban areas, local conditions add complexity to the process. In my firm, the approval of a set of drawings is always a cause for celebration. Once drawings are approved by the local jurisdiction, the design and documentation process is complete… construction is ready to start! From initial discussions of design ideas to the final touches of the completed built project, residential design and construction requires constant coordination between parties.

DIYs beware

I often hear that homeowners can benefit financially from completing stages of the construction process themselves. My answer is always "yes, but…" There are layers of coordination between trades that can be affected by the occasional – and inexperienced – participation of the owner. The main role of the general contractor in building a project is the coordination between trades, from excavation to the final coat of paint. Plumbers and carpenters, electricians and painters, each trade must align with the completed work of the previous tradesperson for the project to avoid delay and waste. Proper staffing, quality work, and an uninterrupted construction development is more economical than the one disrupted by inexperience and lack of coordination between personnel.

When the homeowner participates as an external actor in the construction of the project, it introduces a variety of work quality that needs to be compensated by other trades. This participation has the potential to affect timeline of staffing, void warranties, and damage completed work. In my experience, the homeowner has better chances to participate in the construction by completing stages of the work that are detached from others. For example, the assembly of kitchen cabinetry is time consuming but easy to complete outside of the construction site. By putting together the cabinets, the client contributes time and resources to the project without interfering with the critical path of other trades. Once the cabinets are assembled, the contractor can bring them onto the site and continue with the completion of the kitchen.

Because personal touches contribute to a sense of ownership, I suggest that homeowners participate in construction by introducing individual elements and choices that have an aesthetic influence in the project but will not interfere with the operation of the building. For example, applied colors like paint and wallpaper, finishing touches like art, or even curtains. There are a lot of options where including personal work into a dwelling unit adds character, contributes time, and does not interfere with the critical timeline of the construction process. When the construction process is managed with experience, the contribution of the homeowner can reduce the cost of the building and create personalized touches to the building.

Soft vs hard costs

How much does it all cost? This is one of the first questions discussed during initial calls with potential clients. Every project is affected by its size, location, and complexity, but to understand the final cost of a building, it must be separated into two large groups: soft and hard costs.

Hard costs are those related to materiality of the project, such as supplies and labor costs. Informally called "brick and mortar costs," hard costs have a broad regional variability. In the United States, hard costs tend to be more expensive in the north-east region and less so in the south-east.

Soft costs, on the other hand, are expenses associated with design and permit fees. They are representative of the value to design and document the project in anticipation of construction. Architects, engineers, and lenders contribute to the soft costs of a project, along with permit fees. In general, this part of the building expense is a percentage of the total construction cost. Depending on the region and project, the soft costs of a project can account for 10% to 15% of the total project cost.

Local expertise in design and construction contributes to shorter timelines and reduced soft and hard costs. Collaboration between the design team and clients creates opportunities for savings throughout the development of the project.

The economy of good design

Growing up in a family of carpenters, engineers, and architects, I have always considered the construction industry as accessible as dentists and accountants. Back in Argentina, architects and engineers are contributors of residential projects of all sizes, from small residential additions to multistory buildings. However, I quickly learned that the United States has distanced architects from small-scale design of affordable housing alternatives. Far from a luxury service, architects have the potential to optimize the use of urban space, contribute alternative design options, and offer economic alternatives to housing needs. As architects, we have the opportunity to be proactive participants in the creation of innovative housing options by understanding the scope, timeline and budget of each project.

Initial ideas that contribute to the economy of a project is the project site. By analyzing the location of the building on the property, the architect assists in understanding how, who and for how long a project will serve a homeowner. The siting of a project will enhance the use of the land, the potential for access, and the optimization of energy of the resulting mass.

Because the architect also determines the shape and layout of the structure, the massing of the house will be established by footprint, height, and the orientation of a building. Early decision of the mass of the building will condition options for internal and external accessibility and adaptation to the environment.

Aside from siting and massing, the architect contributes to the economy of the project by designing its exterior envelope. Considered the "skin" that separates the interior from the outdoors, its construction contributes privacy, security, natural light, and sustainable features during the life of the structure.

A building that is properly sited, shaped, and oriented consumes less energy to operate. Aside from siting and massing, good design enriches the experience of interior space. The location, distribution, and organization of rooms contribute to long-term and effective use of the building.

Good design is also economic by anticipating future needs. The size of a patio and its connections to the public way can convert into an electric charging station for a future vehicular needs. A roof installed today with the proper slope can provide the optimal orientation for photovoltaic panels in the future. Residential design that is attuned to the current needs of a client also allows for future additions and alternations.

Construction methods: from traditional to prefabrication

But once the house is designed, can't we just have it built? Can't we buy the building online and have it delivered? We have explored before how a building cost can be broken down into soft and hard costs, also how those hard costs can be divided into systems. Now, why is the assembly of a house so complicated? The construction of a building responds to a method, that is, the type and process of assembly of separate materials. From drywall to doors, from cladding to gutters, the method of construction anticipates a place, process, and cost that outlines how and where those elements are put together. From the factory to the construction site, there is more than one way to assemble a building.

When comparing construction methods to each other, it is important to highlight their contribution to the overall cost of the project. How it affects time of construction, how much it costs to transport, how complex it is to assemble, and the demand for a specialized workforce.

Innovation in home design and construction evolves to satisfy the current deficit in affordable units. The development of new construction methods for alternative housing has given rise to a new set of challenges and benefits.

Construction methods are the result of centuries of development of materials and technologies. Below I organize methods of construction based on the amount of time and distance between individual parts and a complete building. From traditional to modular, there are advantages and disadvantages of each process. This brief recap brings up the potential consequences of choosing one method over another considering cost, time, and long-term implications to the complete project.

The traditional construction method is the process through which a project is assembled on site where each individual trade contributes materials in linear fashion. The materials required for this method are widely available and it requires minimal specialized workforce and equipment to perform it. Materials are delivered on site as required and assembled into the structure. There is minimum space required to stockpile materials because, as products come in, they get incorporated into the building.

The quality of the resulting project will depend on the planning, design, and coordinated implementation of the construction documents. The traditional method allows for custom design ideas, a wide variety of aesthetic choices, and low cost of alterations in the long term. Due to site specific conditions, weather is a contributor to delays. This method is popularly known as "stick built" and is used in contrast to prefabricated construction. Materials of traditional construction are the result of centuries of construction experience. Traditional materials are commercially available and do not require special skills or tools to install and repair.

The biggest advantage of traditional construction is the ease of coordination of different parts. For example, an electrical box, with its $3^3/_4$" of blue plastic, has the perfect depth to attach to a $3^1/_2$" wood stud that will receive a $^1/_2$" thick layer of drywall on top. From stairs to windows, insulation to masonry, elements of traditional construction are already designed to work together on site to avoid material waste and increase speed to assemble. The universality of construction materials, details, and systems in the market today is designed to satisfy the requirements of the traditional construction method.

The economy of traditional construction is strongly associated to the availability and experience of local contractors, the efficient use of available materials, and the ease of transport. Despite its advantages, the biggest disadvantage of traditional construction methods is the coordination of work between trades for an efficient timeline.

Along with traditional construction, prefabrication incorporates preassembled elements into the construction process. While traditional construction is 100% built on site, manufactured housing – in whole or in parts – offers levels of production that can be broken down in components.

In the method of prefabrication called "kit homes" the project results from the selection of a kit of parts that can be assembled on site. Assembling homes from a limited selection of elements was popularized by Sears & Roebuck with their catalogs. The famous "Sears Homes" built between 1908 and 1940 were assembled from a kit of parts available for assembly by anyone, anywhere. This catalog system of housing parts allowed for a level of aesthetic customization but little room for design decisions such as room sizes or climate orientation.

Aside from the historical approach of houses-by-catalog, today there are several levels of preconstruction popular in residential construction. One of them is panelized construction where a building envelope is created by erecting manufactured walls which are attached to foundations on site. The panels are custom cut based on an individual design with openings ready to hold windows and doors. Depending on the manufacturer, the walls contain infrastructure such as electrical and plumbing. Panelized construction creates a load-bearing, insulated building envelope ready to receive custom finishes. All materials that are not included in the prefabrication of the building envelope will come from the traditional construction method. Panelized construction does not include systems such as finishes or infrastructure.

Depending on the manufacturer, panelized construction requires the application of finishes, such as exterior siding or paint, to be completed on site. This method of construction introduces the big challenge of the traditional method: weather. Panelized construction requires design and planning efforts even before the manufacturing of the walls can being while offering limited options for future alterations of the completed building.

Different from the panelized method, modular construction is the process of assembling a building in a factory. The buildings are produced in modules that, once arrived on site, are placed together using a crane to be attached to foundations and infrastructure connections. Modular projects have the opportunity to introduce quality control measures under an assembly line process in the factory and shorten the construction time spent on site. Weather becomes less of a factor in the critical time of construction because the module delivered on site is enclosed and protected from the elements.

Most modular preconstruction methods today deliver portions of each building system: envelope, structure, infrastructure, and finishes. Because none of these systems can operate separately from its site, the cost of the incomplete project must be compensated with the materials and methods of traditional construction. For example, the building envelope and its structure requires connections to the foundations. The walls can be prebuilt in a factory, but the concrete foundations must be poured on site. The point of connections between both elements requires expertise and knowledge of both systems; lack of coordination between traditional and preconstruction systems adds cost and delays.

The interior walls of a modular housing unit will still have to receive paint, tile, and even electrical covers for the outlets. All those elements, even if installed in the factory, will have to survive intact the transportation and assembly efforts on site. Added cost to repair and replace fragile materials damaged on the road, like windows, insulation, and infrastructure, introduces unforeseen costs that may result in significant expense.

Another disadvantage of modular preconstruction is the need to provide for special transportation trucks and cranes for assembly. Urban lots surrounded by tight alleys and limited points of access present additional challenges: oversized trucks demand space to maneuver and cranes are difficult to park. Moreover, in residential construction, equipment operators are one of the highest paid trades. The cost savings of modular homes are offset by the cost implications of transport, assembly, and specialized equipment and personnel required to complete the project on site.

Aside from innovative modular preconstruction methods, manufactured housing is a factory-built unit constructed on a steel chassis and delivered on site to be connected to existing utilities. Manufactured units, also known as mobile homes, have few aesthetic exterior options and a negative social connotation. Their on-site installation is based on land-lease options and available utility connections. They are not installed on foundations and their implementation is limited to the availability of leasing options in the region. Also, not all manufactured housing provides structural safety in extreme weather conditions.

In many regions, zoning laws restrict the placement of manufactured housing in cities. Arguments of this ban range from lot sizes, density of units and aging of the structures. A common ban of manufactured housing in urban environments is related to structural and infrastructure setups. The structural is related to the lack of foundations of manufactured housing as proof that they do not create permanent housing, these units are technically "detached" from the ground. Also, infrastructure connections for mobile homes like water, waste, and electricity contribute to the perception that these units do not constitute safe and sanitary conditions.

From the traditional construction method to innovative modular housing, there are levels of efficiency and economy with each system. Similar to the Sears homes but from a wider variety of options, homes can be assembled by understanding which manufactured parts can be ordered from catalogs. Stairs are a good example on how the off-site preconstruction of building parts contributes aesthetic variety, manufactured precision, and efficiency.

Historically, the construction of a stair was developed by a local carpenter by customizing each riser, tread, and railing to be assembled on site. Today, homeowners can preorder semi-custom stairs, from finished treads, risers, and the structural carriage that will support it. Railings can also be selected from a catalog of aesthetic choices. These separate elements are manufactured off site and delivered to the project following specific dimensions. These products are pre-engineered, finished, and ready to be installed and used.

This type of preassembling of elements saves time, improves quality of construction, and avoids delays. The stair can be ordered from the manufacturer as soon as the framing of the house is complete. It can be delivered on site by a regular sized truck and unloaded by hand. The preordered stair can be installed and assembled on site without the need for specialized equipment, tools, or expertise. From kitchen cabinets to windows and fireplaces, prefabricated construction elements delivered in parts contribute to quality and speed of the project while maintaining adaptability to traditional building methods.

By understanding construction methods, financial options, and building systems, it is evident that the economy and affordability of alternative housing like additional dwelling units is not just dependent on the materiality of a building. Larger factors such as the cost of land, zoning overregulation, and lack of financial options still have a larger impact on the availability of affordable housing in a region.

CHAPTER 7

The Future of Housing

Today is the future of housing

New housing typologies follow new family formats and a demanding economic reality. The future of housing must be created within layers of private and public space to create a supportive environment. The future of single-family homes is transforming from less single-family and more collaborative between neighbors. The home of the future is efficient and effective in its use of space and it welcomes residents in all stages of life. It accommodates individuals with different physical and cognitive abilities to engage in civic participation.

The future of housing is heterogeneous and a promoter of safe and affordable options. It includes more villages and additional dwelling units that foster collaboration and social support. With shared amenities and features, future units are beneficial for families of different economic and cultural backgrounds.

Communal use of outdoor spaces, shared parking, and proximity to transit provide privacy while contributing layers of semi-spaces. The future of housing promotes independent living, self-agency, and is accessible to public services.

The pandemic of 2020 reframed housing as shelter and emphasized a flexible approach to use of space – private and public. Home is, and will always be, the most significant space for individuals to build a sense of belonging and safety. Innovative typologies are the most relevant measure in the future exploration of housing options to compensate for the current dehumanizing deficit.

The public realm, and how the private space reconnects to its surroundings, is the organizer of every other social dynamic. From education to access to healthcare, affordable housing results from a contributing relationship between all tangible and intangible factors of the built environment.

The future of housing must balance the effects of data that can anticipate social and cultural needs for space. From policy makers to architects, professionals and homeowners have the capacity to contribute to affordable and sustainable housing.

The future of housing is today.

About the Author

Ileana Schinder is an architect in Washington, DC. She graduated with a Bachelor's in Architecture from Universidad Nacional de Cordoba (2000, Argentina), and an M.A. in Communications from the American University (2006, Washington, DC).

Inspired to become an architect at the age of four by playing with Lego on the floor, she remains motivated to design houses of all sizes 40 years later. Since opening her architecture studio in 2014, with creativity and innovation, she has designed additional dwelling units that create new spaces for clients and their families to thrive. As part of her effort to educate the public on housing issues, Ileana has also written in blogs and held educational sessions to inspire and promote innovative models of home.

Ileana was born and raised in Argentina. She lives in Washington, DC, with her family and their dog, Cecilia.